# Weaving Strength,
# Weaving Power

# Weaving Strength, Weaving Power

*Violence and Abuse against Indigenous Women*

Venida S. Chenault

PRAIRIE BAND POTAWATOMI AND KICKAPOO

CAROLINA ACADEMIC PRESS

Durham, North Carolina

Library of Congress Cataloging-in-Publication Data

Chenault, Venida S.
Weaving strength, weaving power : violence and abuse against In-
digenous women / Venida S. Chenault.
    p. cm.
Includes bibliographical references and index.
ISBN 978-1-59460-563-5 (alk. paper)
    1. Indian women--United States--Social conditions. 2. Indian
women--Violence against--United States. 3. Indian women--
Abuse of--United States. 4. Indian women--United States--Statis-
tics. 5. Social surveys--United States. 6. Indians of North Amer-
ica--United States--Social conditions. 7. Indians of North
America--Colonization--United States. 8. Imperialism--Social as-
pects--United States. 9. Sex role--United States. 10. Male domination (Social structure)--United States. I. Title.
    E98.W8C47 2011
    305.48'897073--dc22
                        2010043265


CAROLINA ACADEMIC PRESS
700 Kent Street
Durham, North Carolina 27701
Telephone (919) 489-7486
Fax (919) 493-5668
www.cap-press.com

# Contents

# Acknowledgments

I thank Creator for the many blessing you have bestowed upon me and give thanks to all of the traditional people for the prayers, ceremonies and teachings you carry out to ensure the survival and future of our children, our grandchildren and our People. I thank the grassroots scholars and activists, the traditional knowledge bearers, tribal practitioners and Indigenous women who live with and have overcome violence and abuse for sharing your stories and your wisdom. You demonstrate our hearts are not on the ground.

I give thanks for the support of the many tribal people who inspired me to follow in their path and to speak on behalf of those whose voices are never heard. You have taught me to take back my power and to be courageous despite the obstacles encountered in this work of decolonization.

I acknowledge those who mentored, supported and encouraged me during my doctoral program and the visiting scholar appointment which enabled me to complete this book, including the research support of the Prairie Band Potawatomi Nation and the American Indian College Fund.

I especially acknowledge the sacrifice, support and inspiration of my children; the love and support of my immediate, extended and adopted family; as well as my dear friends and colleagues who stood with me in exile for speaking truth to power. I give special thanks to my mother and grandmother for teaching me to be strong and determined and continuing to watch over us.

May those who work for social justice, as well as their families, always be blessed. Igwien.

# Introduction

*Indigenous populations are composed of existing descendants of the peoples who inhabited the present territory of a country wholly or partially at the time when persons of a different culture or ethnic origin arrived there from other parts of the world, overcame them, and, by conquest, settlement or other means, reduced them to a non-dominant or colonial condition ...* (United Nations, 1972).

It can be very difficult for those whose perspective of Indigenous Peoples has been primarily informed by the occasional media story, an image in a movie, a parody of tribal experience in a music video, or the occasional paragraph in a public school text, to move beyond the one-dimensional caricatures, stereotypes, and myths that often inform societal attitudes and beliefs about First Nations People in the United States. Equally challenging is the daunting task confronting tribal leaders, scholars, activists, researchers, and practitioners who devote their expertise and lives to advancing Indigenous sovereignty and self-determination in arenas dominated by legacies of anti-Indianism.[1] A general public that is largely uninformed or misinformed is an absent ally in the discourse shaping public opinion, perceptions, and change

---

1. Cook-Lynn (2007) advanced the concept of *anti-Indianism*, which describes practices, policies, and attitudes that displace and exclude Indigenous People for the purposes of socially isolating, expunging or expelling, defaming, or repulsing Indigenous People in order to control lands, resources, and First Nations.

in the larger society, hindering First Nations. It is not uncommon for college students and professors in the most revered institutions of higher education, state and federal legislators, judges throughout the court systems, and educated professionals in every discipline to be fully uninformed or woefully misinformed about the history, experiences, and unique political status of Indigenous Peoples. Others who argue that 'the past is the past' have simply grown accustomed to the privilege gained by the politics of oppression and are unwilling to give up the advantage created by unjust structures of disparity that remain today. This reality exists while non-tribal decision-makers in multiple systems serving at various levels contemplate issues and render opinions affecting the political and cultural survival of Indigenous Nations using the same colonial systems, laws, and processes historically used to usurp the lands, power, and resources of First Nations and to justify the degradation and deprivation of Indigenous Peoples ignored for generations. The invisibility and continued political struggles of First Nations to exist as constitutionally sovereign and treaty-based Peoples bear witness to the Indigenous legacy of colonialism in the United States, as well as to the corrosive and ongoing effects of colonization. These effects are found in a litany of destabilizing social problems produced by colonialism-induced disruption throughout the social structures of tribal people, including, but not limited to, alcoholism and drug abuse, disproportionate incarceration rates, and soaring levels of violence, suicide, poverty, and unemployment.

The need for research and scholarship focused on pressing issues identified by and with tribal peoples provides an invaluable resource to tribal governments, communities, and organizations as solution-oriented strategies are developed for retaining political rights, advancing tribal interests, and building capacity in communities devastated by the genocidal practices, policies, and laws of colonialism. *Weaving Strength, Weaving Power,* focuses on the Indigenous experience of colonization and the contemporary manifestation of this experience in violence and abuse against Indigenous women, as well as the dysfunctional systems and mindsets that enable oppression to continue. *Social justice,* as defined in structural social work scholarship,[2] is committed to "the elimination of institutionalized domination and oppression,"[3] an approach essential for addressing the multidimensional issues facing Indigenous Peoples. This philosophic approach is cognizant of the structural dynamics that undergird injustice and is especially relevant to examination of Indigenous colonization. This conceptualization of *social justice* best describes parallel work within the discipline of Native Studies, or *Indigenous Studies*, as will be used here. The discipline of Indigenous Studies is characterized by frameworks, models, approaches, and practices supporting the advancement of sovereign Indigenous Nations, including the dissemination of research and scholarship addressing tribal priorities and needs. Advocacy and social action at multiple levels are the tools for social change relevant to this discipline, as well as relevant for social justice practitioners. Seeking to overcome a long history of subjugation, new generations of Indigenous agents of change are engaged in intentional efforts to resolve a legacy of entrenched structural imbalance and systemic dysfunction diverting the potential of tribal communities. Using the knowledge, experiences, and political status retained by Indigenous Nations and Peoples, whenever possible, these proponents of change are weaving existing knowledge with innovative new strategies and research-based scholarship in campaigns to overcome the legacy of colonization and subjugation in order to ensure the survival of Indigenous cultures, worldviews, philosophies, and hopefulness for the future of tribal peoples.

The history of Indigenous Peoples documents the catastrophic disruption and damage produced by imperialism and colonialism.

---

2. Mullaly's scholarship, *Structural Social Work: Ideology, Theory, and Practice* (1997), advances the position that the primary focus of structural social work is to end oppression. The emphasis of this approach is consistent with similar positions within the discipline of Indigenous Studies, particularly the 2007 work of Elizabeth Cook-Lynn, *New Indians, Old Wars*.

3. This stance is grounded in the work of Iris Marion Young's 1990 book, *Justice and the Politics of Difference*, as well as Barry D. Adam's 1978 analysis of internalized oppression in *The Survival of Domination: Inferiorization in Everyday Life* as discussed by Mullaly (1997, p. 140).

Too often this history and these experiences are approached as if there were no impact on the people, the structures, or the systems that exist in the civilizations of Indigenous Nations. Approaches cognizant of systemic disruption and the dynamics of disempowerment on First Nations are critical to capacity- or nation-building efforts. Little progress can be achieved without acknowledgement of both this history and the necessary engagement with change processes: first, acknowledging this history in creating social and structural disruption, and second, acknowledging the use of change processes that engage communities — devastated by practices of subjugation — in self-determination as next steps are identified. Linking such approaches with the knowledge and political status retained by Indigenous Nations and with the experiences, strengths, resources, and capacity within tribal communities ensures a strong foundation for this work. Indigenous social justice is a convergence of such intent with the work of Indigenous Studies, described by eminent Native Studies scholar, Elizabeth Cook-Lynn as a sacred responsibility that is situated in the indigenousness and sovereignty of First Nations.[4]

The external forces that set colonialism into motion represent just one dimension of change, but additional layers must also be addressed. Equally important is the acknowledgement of the extent to which this history and the associated practices of oppression have disrupted traditional cultures, knowledge, and systems and have been consciously and unconsciously adopted by American Indians. Not only must individual tribal members be held accountable, but also tribal governments, communities, and organizations that benefit from the adoption of attitudes and practices of domination to ensure the elimination of institutionalized domination and oppression within each arena of Indigenous Nations.

*Weaving Power, Weaving Strength* examines the disruptive interpersonal and structural effect of colonialism on Indigenous social structures, particularly the debilitating consequences on gendered systems and knowledge, as well as the traditional cultural teachings and gen-

---

4. Cook-Lynn (2007).

dered practices. Violence and abuse against Indigenous women is approached as a manifestation of the collapse and disruption of structures and cultural systems valuing women. *Structural approaches* are contrary to *victim-blaming approaches,* which situate causation in the individual or culture without any examination of the structural forces or conditions that contribute to social problems.

A *structural approach* expands the analysis to consider the multilayered and interlocking effects of structural disruption on social systems, organizations, and functioning throughout the civilizations of Indigenous Peoples. This approach focuses both on the social change that engages those affected by existing conditions and on the utilization of existing strengths and capacity for doing so. By incorporating a gendered structural analysis of colonialism, the role of the multidimensional dynamics of colonization in the oppression of Indigenous women can be considered to ensure that systemic and culturally relevant solutions are advanced for violence and abuse against Indigenous women. Clearly, the subjugation of Indigenous Nations at every level, and in every system, must also be challenged if the desired goal of social justice is to be fully achieved on Indigenous terms.

*Weaving Power, Weaving Strength* is a product of a sustained Indigenous movement of sociopolitical change, inspired by a long history of grassroots activism and many generations of fiercely independent and strong tribal people who mentor and motivate emerging First Nations scholars, practitioners, and researchers to consciously confront oppression and injustice through the revitalization of Indigenous knowledge. While this book addresses the disturbing problem of violence and abuse against Indigenous women, the approach may be equally valuable in examining other systemic social problems associated with colonialism-induced structural disruption.

This book connects strengths, empowerment, and structural approaches from social work with the concepts of sovereignty, self-determination, and indigenousness from Indigenous Studies as a basis for Indigenous social justice that seeks to end the institutionalized domination and oppression of Indigenous Nations. This work intentionally links interdisciplinary research with the renegade research and wisdom of grassroots Indigenous scholars and practitioners, whose contributions have been historically marginalized by mainstream systems. Such approaches are consistent with Indigenous worldviews and philosophies of interconnectedness versus disconnection. Those seeking a fragmented disciplinary approach, a simplistic 'cookie-cutter' method for fixing violence against women, or a template that relies on deficit approaches will be greatly disappointed.

Colonialism is approached as the trigger for massive structural disruption and system collapse throughout the civilizations and social organizations of Indigenous Nations. Evidence of the destabilization produced by these calamitous changes is wide-ranging; however, this examination considers the example of violence and abuse against Indigenous women. Violence and abuse against women is an adopted behavior that contradicts the traditional cultural worldviews and philosophies and the instructions found in emergence narratives, as well as the practices inherent to the gendered systems, knowledge, and teachings of tribal peoples. Rather than viewing violence against women as an isolated phenomenon, an integrated analysis of the source of corruption of gendered systems and practices that uphold Indigenous cultures are considered as key factors in the destabilization of tribal cultures and social disruption affecting Indigenous Nations today.

Violence against Indian women is without doubt an attack on tribal women, but it also represents a continued assault on the traditional cultures of tribal peoples that maintain very different philosophies about the power, place, and value of Indigenous women. By reconnecting to and utilizing the strengths of the traditional cultures, the wisdom of the origin narratives, the gendered teachings within these creation stories, and the systems and processes that support strong tribal women, the full power of Indigenous Peoples is embraced. The use of culturally based solutions become powerful steps toward the reclamation and revitalization of gendered wisdom — as reflected by commonly acknowledged Cheyenne saying: *A Nation is not defeated until the hearts of its women are on the ground* — and toward the perpetuation of cultures that must be lived in order to be saved.

The importance of connecting knowledge from seemingly disparate academic disciplines in order to understand the contemporary phenomenon of violence against Indigenous women will be problematic for some, but it is appropriate from an Indigenous orientation and integral to structural analysis. While this connection poses challenges within the academy about proscribed disciplinary boundaries, an interdisciplinary approach lends itself to examination of the multifarious nature of colonization and its layered effects on structures and systems throughout the cultures of Indigenous Nations. Broadly speaking, *systems and interdisciplinary approaches* typically consider the interactions and relationships within and between multiple systems, as well as the interactions of these smaller systems within a larger structure and the effects of such throughout these connected systems. These approaches recognize that *change produces more change*, both intended and unintended at every level, from the micro (smallest) to macro (largest) levels of systems. It has been long recognized, for example, that rapid social change that does not provide for meaningful participation in the changes being made and that inadequate time to prepare for or adjust to change can be disruptive on multiple levels, including a loss of meaning as beliefs and practices are lost. The emergence of practices inconsistent with former worldviews, beliefs, and practices is not unusual when voids are not filled with what is meaningful. Behaviors acquired that are inconsistent with traditional teachings and norms often produce discord at multiple levels. As one considers the historical effect of imposed changes resulting from colonialism, a potential shift in the analysis of impact is possible by linking the knowledge about human behavior, community organization, and the dynamics of change into the equation.

*Systems theory* or *structural frameworks* are typically not attributed to Indigenous Peoples; however, it is argued here these approaches are evident within the Indigenous worldviews and cultural philosophies. Within tribal systems, there is both a recognition of and respect for the myriad of multilayered relationships within a variety of systems, both human and non-human. This type of thinking is common across tribes, including the well-known Lakota acknowledgment, *mitake oyasin (all are related)*, which honors the ways we are connected and related to all of life. If one believes that all are related and connected to human and non-human entities, that all have purpose, and that all are equally valued within the cosmos, such a worldview fundamentally alters decisions, attitudes, and practices. Such perspectives enable one to appreciate basic concepts of Indigenous worldviews, which promote connectedness rather than disconnection and equality of life versus inequality. Again, these beliefs of traditional Indigenous Peoples are important to consider in examination of how Indigenous Nations that value and respect women have reached the point at which violence and abuse against Indigenous women is a growing epidemic, as well as important in investigation of what is needed to correct this dysfunction.

Tribal philosophies are acquired, memorialized, and reinforced in innumerable practices of Indigenous People to ensure that these relationships and connections are acknowledged, honored, and restored as needed. Acquiring wisdom about the significance of the many teachings occurs over the course of a lifetime and comes from listening to, observation of, participation in, and living the beliefs of tribal peoples. Theories of origin or emergence narratives are the basis for the worldviews and philosophies of a given People and often provide the 'instructions for life'. These processes of socialization ensure one develops an appreciation and comprehension of the layers of knowledge within the traditional cultures, worldviews, and philosophies of tribal peoples that provide a cultural basis for life.

*Indigenous system thinking* is also founded on the use of a long-term or generational perspective that considers the impacts of decisions and actions on future generations, both human and non-human, often referred to as *seven generations philosophies*. Even in the approach to the issue of violence and abuse against Indigenous women, one does so thinking about the future generations of women being born and prepared to assume pivotal roles in advancing the survival and sovereignty of Indigenous Nations. The traditional decision-making processes within Indigenous Nations are characterized by deliberative and consensual processes for input and an approach that relies on the connection to the sacred for guidance. These processes are also generally characterized by inclusionary versus exclusionary approaches to ensure that all voices are represented in the deliberations, especially those of women. As cultures that recognize the textured and profound intersections between human, natural, and spiritual systems and the cosmos, attention is given to the consequences of actions and changes being made, particularly those with the potential for disrupting hardship. This recognition of—and respect for—the relationships and systems that exist between all elements of Creation is embedded throughout these cultures and interwoven throughout the traditional cultures, systems, beliefs, behaviors, attitudes, and practices of First Nations. Disturbances within systems or the foundations of a culture, which produce discord or imbalance, are viewed as problematic when functioning is disrupted. **This recognition of the concept of *interconnectedness* and the need to maintain a balance within Creation is the fundamental foundation of Indigenous worldviews, spirituality, and practices in which every element of Creation is honored and acknowledged to ensure balance is maintained and restored if needed.** Although these ways of thinking, as well as the systems and structures promoting such practices have been under siege during much of the history of Indigenous colonization in the United States, they have never been fully crushed.

Indigenous empowerment models predicated on sovereignty and indigenousness—emphasizing the inherent right to utilize tribal cultures, knowledge, systems, and practices in responses and initiatives at multiple levels—are increasingly used by tribal Nations confronting injustice across many domains. Communities and organizations dedicated to cultural revitalization and capacity-building on Indigenous terms, are incorporating parallel strategies that contemplate the effects on sovereignty and embrace the inherent tribal right to determine approaches in overcoming these legacies of oppression. These approaches are increasingly common to tribally based programs responding to violence against Indigenous women.

Traditionally, tribal women were not relegated to a second-class or inferior status within the systems of tribal peoples. In fact, such approaches are antithetical to the canons found in the aforementioned traditional cultural philosophies and beliefs. Strong women and female deities, equally powerful in the cultures of Indigenous Peoples, abound in the theories of origin, teachings, lessons of survival, and rich experiences of tribes. Gendered beliefs and philosophies that retain these ways of thinking are embedded in the cultural teachings, in the daily and ceremonial practices, and in the systems operating throughout these civilizations, which often still exist among many tribes today. An orientation that bespeaks the respect that traditional tribal peoples hold for gender, including women and female powers within Creation, is invaluable to systemic solutions for violence and abuse against Indigenous women. For many, the 2009 Indigenous Bolivian delegation's successful lobby to the United Nations to recognize *Earth Day* as *Mother Earth Day* was unnoticed; however, to others, this important symbolic change was a significant and long overdue shift in honoring and acknowledging the relationships with the original Mother. Actions that change consciousness about the relationships and responsibilities between human and non-human entities produce the potential for changing worldviews and philosophies of domination and oppression, including the subjugation of women by violence and abuse and marginalization within First Nations and Mother Earth.

Unfortunately, the right of traditional Indigenous Peoples to protect the First Mother and her sacred sites or to carry out cultural responsibilities divinely vested with First Nations is continually challenged by litigation and a litany of genocidal rules, laws, and regulations that interfere with the traditional religious and cultural practices of Indigenous Peoples today. Worldwide, many First Nations People view the collective ignorance, greed, hubris, and lack of regard for traditional philosophies and practices of Indigenous Peoples as contributing to imbalance on many levels, with the dissonant practices and attitudes towards women and female power providing further evidence of the discord produced by philosophies steeped in male entitlement and subjugation.

Today bears witness to the multiple layers of disruption and imbalance worldwide, set into motion by the ancient structural forces of imperialism and colonialism. The global consequences are evident of the massive sociocultural structural disruption and turmoil predicated on worldviews and philosophies of domination and oppression. These philosophies have triggered global disruption in social organizations by privileging male-dominated hierarchical systems to the exclusion of egalitarian and gendered systems valuing women. The unprecedented level of horrific violence and abuse against women, girls, and female infants throughout the world is but one example of the imbalance produced. There are no women or female children who are immune from violence and abuse or the corrosive effects of changes that have occurred over history in regard to the treatment and respect for women. One must ask why the female population—of every nation, of every religion, of every social class—must live in fear of violence and abuse, for being born female. Too often, attention is diverted away from the structural dynamics that tolerate, promote, and profit from the oppression of women and girls globally and the insidious processes of desensitization to institutionalized violence against the female population, as well as other disenfranchised populations. There is nothing just in blaming women and girls for the violence and abuse they experience in order to protect the profits of capitalism, regimes of misogynistic intolerance, or politics of domination and oppression.

The monumental task of addressing Indigenous issues, including nation-building and advocating on behalf of Indigenous Peoples, requires evaluation of the multidimensional and interlocking dimensions of colonialism and imperialism confronted by First Nations People and the role of these forces in spawning institutionalized domination and oppression. Pawnee scholar, Julia Goodfox, describes decolonization as a "process of reconnection"[5] to the strength of philosophies, knowledge, systems, and practices of First Nations that have served tribal people over millenniums. Such understandings are instrumental to Indigenous empowerment and the survival of tribal cultures. Multiple levels of reconnection are essential to capacity-building within Indigenous Nations, including within individuals and families and between communities, organizations, social systems, governments, and Nations, both tribal and non-tribal.

---

5. Goodfox (personal conversation, 2009).

The work required does not end with becoming conscious of how the current state of affairs has been reached — instead it requires proactive social change to reverse and end the damage done at every level and to renew the connections to Indigenous knowledge and practices. Institutionalized philosophies, worldviews, and practices of domination and oppression must be critically evaluated at every level and countered with responses that build on the strengths, resources, and capacities found within Indigenous cultures, knowledge, worldviews, philosophies, practices, and experiences. The history and experience of Indigenous Nations must be acknowledged and considered as solutions are advanced to reverse the fragmentation of holistic Indigenous cultures. This movement is about recapturing power and using it to create a future.

Much of the history of federal "Indian" relations, policy, legislation, and regulations is indelibly stained by the failed strategies of annihilation, termination, and assimilation that fundamentally altered the traditional cultures and social structures of Indigenous People, even today. Righting an Indigenous world that has been turned "upside down,"[6] as described by Yupik scholar, Harold Napoleon, requires talking honestly about the truth, yet too often, those advancing progressive research and scholarship find the Indigenous holocaust denied, and find their disciplines, departments, organizations, and professional reputations under siege, particularly within the disciplines of Indigenous Studies and Social Work. Common knowledge holds that speaking truth to power does not always equate with positive decisions about tenure and promotion within institutions of higher education. More recently, the "ethnic studies" legislation passed in the state of Arizona, HB 2281,[7] signed into law by Governor Jan Brewer in April 2010, bans ethnic studies in kindergarten through twelfth-grade schools within the state by prohibiting classes designed for students of particular ethnic groups that promote ethnic solidarity over individualism or that promote resentment toward other groups. This state legislation tar-

---

6. Napoleon (1991, p. 4).
7. State of Arizona (2010).

gets Chicano and Mexican American studies in the Tucson school district and mandates loss of state funding for districts that do not comply. While such programs in colleges and universities are currently exempt, and specific language is included stating that courses or classes for Native American pupils *required to comply with federal law* are exempt, a dangerous precedent has been set for criminalizing ethnic studies, as well as the discipline of Indigenous and American Indian Studies, legitimizing the oppression of cultures and Peoples of Color. The policy declares that public schools students should be taught to treat and value each other as individuals and not be taught to resent or hate other races or classes of people, while legislation outlawing the study of or appreciation for the cultures, histories, experiences, and contributions of Mexican students — as represented by Chicano Studies — are portrayed as subversive.

At the risk of redundancy, the devastating social conditions and problems facing Indigenous Peoples and communities today cannot be fully understood without examining the backdrop of history and the effects of colonialism, imperialism, and colonization on the social systems and fabric of Indigenous Nations. (*Colonization* is defined as the *process phase of colonialism,* as discussed later in text.) These events are the 'elephant in the room' that must be discussed in order to move forward, rather than ignored or denied. It is remarkable that, in 2010, Indigenous People in the United States and throughout the world must still utilize limited resources to resist policies and practices that threaten to further destabilize tribal cultures, languages, homelands, and spiritual practices in order to enjoy the simple freedom of living one's traditional culture without persecution, prosecution, or prostitution, in the broadest sense. The cultures of Indigenous People in the United States are among the most highly regulated but most maligned within the nation. It is unconscionable that energy and resources are effectively diluted or diverted away from the pressing work of nation-building required after centuries of oppression, yet the work of protecting land bases and resuscitating cultures, languages, and traditional practices that are near collapse in some tribes is consistently compromised by the skirmishes and battles in hostile courts and legis-

latures of state and the federal government, as well as the multi-
tude of agencies and institutions with which tribal people engage
daily. Indigenous colonization is alive and well, and some maintain that a new phenomenon of re-colonization is gaining momentum in more repressive organizations and tribal communities,
particularly those aligned with agendas of oppression inherent to
federal "Indian-control" policies. Simultaneously, the race-baiting
rhetoric of conservative pundits and politicians, the acts of domestic terrorism by Right Wing elements, and the violence by those
associated with White Supremacy groups all attack the sovereign
rights and status of Indigenous Nations with a vengeance. Fur-
thermore, such agendas are increasingly promoted through media.
Post-colonial discussions are premature, to say the least.

Socialization practices and socially constructed images of Indigenous People, intended and inadvertent, perpetuated by nations, have powerful influences on the social conditions, perceptions,
and societal attitudes of individuals, communities, and groups at
multiple levels. To ignore the influence of these societal and structural forces is problematic. The unquestioning belief in what one
has been taught—or, conversely, not been taught—through the institutions of a society can be so commanding that many of the most
destructive and ingrained opinions, attitudes, and beliefs about Indigenous Nations and other diverse populations are not easily corrected. The general public is not immune from acquiring the attitude
and belief that certain groups are superior to others or from de-
fending the privilege that comes with such status, even at this junc-
ture in history. Those within diverse communities historically
targeted by such practices are also not invulnerable to the toxic effects of internalizing their oppression and acting accordingly or
even becoming participants in the oppression and dominations of
others.

This book is intended to move beyond the victim-blaming approaches of the past. It unapologetically embraces the strength of
the cultural knowledge and teachings of First Nations People and
the power of indigenousness inherent to this experience. It is intended
to advance critical examination and discussion about violence
against Indigenous women throughout diverse domains including

the escalating violence, particularly for young tribal women. This book cannot and is not intended to represent all perspectives, to answer every question, or to solve the problem worldwide, but is instead intended to engage the passion of others committed to Indigenous women, empowerment, and social justice to approach the issue from a different orientation.

*Weaving Strength, Weaving Power* is written from the perspective of Indigenous eyes and is about working with people who have been historically marginalized and disillusioned by the promises and realities of democracy in America. This book is about the strengths, the resilience, and the processes of empowerment within individuals, families, communities, and Indigenous Nations. The focus is on reclaiming the power that has been stripped away, given away, taken away, tricked away, or never been fully realized, in order to create the needed action and change. The approach may be useful to those with an interest in the Indigenous experience of violence and abuse; in the effect of colonialism on social structures and systems, including gender systems; and in the frameworks for Indigenous empowerment that engage stakeholders determining next steps for social action and change. It recognizes the physical, emotional, spiritual, and interpersonal trauma experienced by women to whom violence and abuse have occurred but also acknowledges the determination and resiliency of Indigenous women to overcome these experiences using approaches valuing traditional tribal knowledge. It builds on the strengths of experiences of tribal women to facilitate the changes needed, in ways that do not require being a victim or even survivor.

Tribal people live and work beside the ordinary citizen, pay taxes, and participate in the democratic processes within tribal communities and the urban areas that serve as home to increasing populations of tribal peoples. In the 21st century, despite the incredible belief of too many, Indigenous People no longer live in teepees in the hinterlands of America, although many reservations are coping with Third World living conditions. Contrary to media hype, the majority of First Nations People are not growing rich from casino enterprises. In fact, the ratio of tribal people who still live in poverty is double that of the total population according to the United States

Census Bureau, many without basic access to running water, electricity, and indoor plumbing.[8] Understanding of the unique political status of Indigenous Peoples, the government-to-government relationship, sovereignty, self-determination, and the sociopolitical experience of First Nations People represents a level of *deep knowledge* that is fundamental for an informed and educated insight into the Indigenous experience. Too often, only those within the circle pursue in-depth study of First Nations: individuals, tribes, and organizations dedicated to advancing social justice and human rights.

Talking honestly about the truth facilitates responses and conditions for individuals, families, communities, and nations to take power back by addressing the issues faced and by engaging in self-determination predicated on choices, including identifying solutions at multiple levels to build capacity or nations. Raising awareness of the dynamics of oppression generates thinking about the ways in which one can engage in resistance to the stereotype, can refuse to acquiesce to oppressive practices, and can reject internalizing tyranny as 'just the way things are.' Rage, hopelessness, and despair are not uncommon when one realizes the magnitude of the challenge faced for the crime of being born Indigenous; however, such circumstances do not justify abandoning tribal cultures by engaging in violence against Indigenous women. Being forced to discard the traditional foundation of cultural knowledge, including the philosophically and spiritually based teachings, values, systems, and practices, is an exercise of cultural genocide producing destabilizing consequences, worsened when the vacuum created is not filled with comparable meaning and relevance. These dynamics should not be equated with hopelessness but instead viewed as consciousness of the complexity of the issues faced within and by Indigenous Peoples and as recognition of the need for multidimensional strategies and solutions based on strengths-based empowerment frameworks.

We are all related—We are all connected.

---

8. United States Census Bureau (2000; 2006, February).

# Weaving Strength, Weaving Power

## Chapter One

# We Are All Related—
# We Are All Connected

> … the advancement of Indigenous Women's human rights
> is inextricably linked to the struggle to protect, respect and
> fulfill both the rights of our Peoples as a whole and our
> rights as women without our communities and at the na-
> tional and international level (1995 Foro Internacional
> de Mujeres Indigenas [FIMI, International Indigenous
> Women's Forum] Beijing + 10 Declaration of Indige-
> nous Women, as cited in FIMI, 2006, p. 17).

Violence and abuse against women is a pervasive, complex, and
global social problem rooted in multiple structural and power dynamics that have evolved over centuries and across civilizations.[1]
The ideologies, attitudes, behaviors, and practices of oppression
at multiple levels, provide unwavering structural support for disempowering acts of violence and abuse against women and many
other groups. Too often analysis of pressing social problems fail to
critique the interlocking dynamics of subjugation or the intersectionality of social structures and power relations in creating, reinforcing, and perpetuating oppressive practices such as violence
against women. Minimizing, ignoring, or denying the influence of

---

1. Numerous scholars from multiple disciplines, including Social Work,
Indigenous Studies, and Women's Studies, increasingly acknowledge the
structural nature of violence and abuse against women and the need to
promote change at this level. The work of Davis, Hagen, & Early (1994),
Moane (1999), Busch & Valentine (2000), Meyer-Emerick (2001), Smith
(2001; 2005), and Denetdale (2009) are among those influencing this body
of scholarship.

these forces ensures the perpetuation of fragmented analyses that too frequently rely on victim-blaming approaches or deficit analysis in the identification of both cause and solutions to social problems, leaving intact the structural dynamics of domination, the systems of domination, and the problems arising from such philosophies. Those subjugated by these conditions, including women who experience violence, too frequently find themselves in the untenable position of being blamed for causing the problem, while choices are lost and oppressive social conditions and systems are ignored, trivialized, justified, and perpetuated.

When violence and abuse occur in communities of color, the dynamics of victim-blaming approaches are layered in ways to include entire communities and cultures and are reinforced by the common presumption that such problems are typical to the dysfunctional communities, the deficient cultures, or the populations represented, and thus are justifiably ignored. Analysis of the structural interplay between sociopolitical forces and multiple systems influencing power relations and perception is necessary for understanding the interactions between systems of oppression, the effect on social conditions, and the development of change strategies addressing these dynamics.

Individuals, families, communities, organizations, and nations that remain unconscious and unaware of the havoc generated by this matrix of oppression are at risk for internalizing paradigms condoning the attitudes, behaviors, and practices of domination, too often normalized within societies. Left unchecked, these systems and the accompanying socialization practices ensure the survival of ancient and unrelenting systems of oppression that place entire segments of society at risk for acquiescing to such conditions. Media campaigns promoting narratives of inferiority and the use of dehumanizing stereotypes influence public opinion and tacitly condone unspoken attitudes, behaviors, and practices justifying racism and oppression. Indigenous women, as well as other marginalized populations, are too often devalued in systems designed to maintain male-dominated hierarchical structures and are consequently at risk.

Social change movements emerging out of the 1960s and 1970s posed a formidable challenge to the prevailing structures of race-, culture-, and gender-based oppression within American society, although it is also true that resistance to these forces of domination existed long before these movements. The alignment of these movements served as a catalyst for broad social change as ideologies, behaviors, attitudes, and practices of oppression embedded within society were protested and consciousness of the structural dynamics of oppression was advanced. It was during this time that the Red Power Movement and the discipline of Native Studies emerged; also, this time was the point at which confrontation of gender-based oppression would set the agenda for the Women's Movement for the next 40 years, with a particular emphasis on violence against women.

Proponents of deficit approaches then and now argue that the examination of conditions and structures that disenfranchise communities and cultures are little more than an effort to blame someone else or something else for the problem, thus allowing individuals to escape blame or personal responsibility for their actions. Rather than engaging in the work required to bring about change in dysfunctional structures and systems, a common refrain of these adherents — 'get over it' — suggests that social structures and conditions of oppression no longer exist and are a vestige of the past, if any history of oppression is ever acknowledged. While persuasive to those who rattle the saber of personal accountability and the crowd that espouses, "Be damned the conditions that surround you, pull yourself up by your bootstraps", these approaches deflect attention from the potent role that systems of privilege and power continue to play in marginalizing and exploiting ordinary citizens, particularly those disenfranchised by status ascribed by factors such as race, class, or gender. Too often evidence of disruption in communities of color resulting from these social conditions and a litany of oppressive social policies becomes fodder used by conservative decision-makers and racist power brokers to bolster longstanding claims of pathology, deficiency and the criminal element within these cultures. Indigenous Nations, as well as ethnic minority groups within the United States have not been immune to these forces, with the heavy toll of victim blaming and the accompanying diversion of resources created by a culture of fear only worsening dire circumstances.

Against this backdrop, the need for a multifaceted and systemic examination of the historic forces of oppression and the relationship between these structural forces and the contemporary phenomenon of violence against Indigenous women would seem evident. Over the past four decades, prevalence data established the scope of the problem and continue to document the pervasiveness of violence against women.[2] Education campaigns generated awareness and support for the establishment of shelters and legislation to protect women experiencing domestic violence and sexual assault. The literature base on violence and abuse against women provided early conceptual insight into the dynamics and impacts of violence, as well as theories and practices on which prevention and intervention are typically based.

Ongoing and mutual efforts at the national, tribal, and state levels generated support for the replication of mainstream criminal justice, law enforcement, and prosecution systems in tribal communities, as well as tougher responses from these systems. These efforts culminated in the passage of the Violence Against Women Act (VAWA) in 1994 and its reauthorization in 2000 by President Bill Clinton (as Division B of the Victims or Trafficking and Violence Protection Act of 2000), followed by its reauthorization again in 2006 by President George W. Bush.[3] While VAWA has been de-

---

2. Numerous studies by the United States Department of Justice, particularly the *American Indians and Crime* reports (1999; 2004) shed light on the prevalence and incidence of violence against Indigenous women, as well as both qualitative and quantitative studies by Chapin (1994), Norton & Manson (1995), Davis, Hagen, & Early (1994), West (1997), Tjaden & Thoennes (1998; 1999; 2000 February; 2000 November), National Institute for Justice (2000), and United States Centers for Disease Control and Prevention (US CDC) (2000).

3. Violence Against Women Act (VAWA) (1994); VAWA—Victims of Trafficking and Violence Protection Act (2000); Violence Against Women and Department of Justice Reauthorization Act (2005). President Bush signed the Violence Against Women Act of 2005 (VAWA 2005) into law on January 5, 2006; the *History of the Violence Against Women Act* is available at http://www.ovw.usdoj.gov/docs/history-vawa.pdf (United States Department of Justice, Office of Violence Against Women [n.d.]).

scribed as the most extensive support given by the federal government to improving, expanding, and enhancing services to women, violence and abuse against women has not ended.

Although all women are affected by gendered oppression, women of color often confront multiple forms of oppression in their lives, including structural violence from the very systems targeted for change by VAWA, as well as lateral violence and abuse within intimate relationships, families, and communities, with little attention or fanfare. According to the February 2006 United States Census Bureau findings, First Nations who identify solely as American Indian and Alaska Native represent 2.7 million people, of which 1.3 million are women, with the population increasing to 4.3 million in combination with one or more other races, of which 2.3 million are women.[4] These women often live with the destructive consequences of multilayered oppression and domination, including violence and abuse.

While it may come as surprise to those whose image of tribal women have been informed by media distortions, violence and abuse against Indigenous women (VAAIW) neither existed or was historically tolerated within tribal communities. Instead, women within the traditional cultures of Indigenous Peoples exercise significant power in multiple arenas of tribal civilizations, as well as the innate right to make decisions about their lives and choices about their own bodies.[5] Today, Indigenous women are disempowered by rates of violence and abuse at epidemic proportions, yet only recently has this phenomenon attracted national attention in both the United States and Canada.[6] Rather than approaching

---

4. United States Census Bureau (2006).

5. Early scholarship on gender and violence within tribal cultures includes Gunn Allen (1992), *The Sacred Hoop: Recovering the Feminine in American Indian Traditions*; Maracle (1996), *I Am Woman: A Native Perspective on Sociology and Feminism*; and Albers and Medicine (1983), *The Hidden Half: Studies of Plains Indian Women*. Most recently, the writing and community-based work of Mohawk activist, Jessica Yee (2009), has focused attention on the effects of colonialism on the reproductive rights of Indigenous women in her blog, *Reclaiming Choice for Native Women*.

6. Indigenous women in Canada are documenting the failure of the Canadian government to acknowledge, investigate, or act on violence

VAAIW as an indicator of individual or cultural deficiency, as the deficit pundits would argue, this phenomenon is better understood as a manifestation of colonialism—the structural disruption produced by this experience and the interlocking dynamics of oppression that operate to maintain this illusion of status quo.

The invasion and subjugation of First Nations Peoples by European colonizers marked the onset of Indigenous colonization in the Americas. The ongoing processes associated with colonization triggered ongoing shifts and disruption within every domain of First Nations cultures, social structures, and organizations, with detrimental effects on the lives and experiences of Indigenous Peoples, including gender. As discussed by Maori scholar, Linda Tuhiwai Smith, the term *gender* describes the roles of both men and women, the way these roles are defined, and the relations between men and women, as defined by cultural traditions of knowledge.[7] The term *gendered structural disruption* is used here to describe *the loss, the collapse, the disruption of, and the repression of traditional societies, practices, and beliefs and systems that function to socialize one into gender roles, responsibilities, and interactions with one another based on Indigenous traditions of knowledge.* The adoption of misogynistic attitudes, behaviors, and practices supporting the oppression and denigration of women through violence and abuse at multiple levels is one example of gender disruption in tribal communities. Today, this disruption is embodied by the contemporary problem of VAAIW in cultures with remarkably different traditional belief systems about power and gender.

Indigenous women are increasingly targeted for a wide range of violence and abuse, both within tribal communities and throughout mainstream society. Tribal communities began responding to the phenomenon of VAAIW in the 1970s. Early anecdotal reports

---

against First Nations women that has resulted in more than 500 Indigenous women missing and murdered in Canada. A 2009 Amnesty International report, *Canada: No More Stolen Sisters: A Human Rights Response to Discrimination and Violence Against Indigenous Women in Canada* documents this injustice.

7. Smith (1999).

of domestic violence estimated 50% to 80% of First Nations women in some community samples experienced such violence.[8] Although these findings were dismissed on the basis of small sample sizes and the anecdotal nature of the findings, they provided preliminary evidence of a level of disruption all but ignored. For nearly two decades after these initial studies, between the 1970s and 1990s, there was an absence of scholarship focusing on VAAIW or the contemporary consequences of gendered disruption emanating from the experience of colonization.

More recent reports such as *American Indians and Crime*,[9] findings from the *National Violence Against Women Survey*,[10] the Amnesty International report *Maze of Injustice*,[11] and the companion report to the United Nations Secretary-General's Study on Violence Against Women, *Mairin Iwanka Raya*,[12] provide startling documentation of the global nature and disproportionate levels of VAAIW. First Nations women in the United States are significantly more likely to report rape, physical assault, and stalking than women of any other racial or ethnic background, according to these studies. The 1999 United States Department of Justice report, *American Indians and Crime*, indicates Indigenous women experience violent crimes at a rate nearly 50% higher than other victims of violence.[13] In 1999 and in 2004, the Department of Justice reported the rate of sexual assault is higher among First Nations women than any other women in the United States; this rate has not changed.[14] Sara Deer, a leading Muscogee (Creek) legal expert on violence crime on reservations reported in 2003 that one in three Indigenous women will be raped during her lifetime;[15] no evidence to date sug-

---

8. Chapin (1994); Norton & Manson (1995); West (1997).
9. United States Department of Justice (1999; 2004).
10. Tjaden & Thoennes (1998; 1999).
11. Amnesty International (2007).
12. Foro Internacional de Mujeres Indígenas (FIMI) [International Indigenous Women's Forum] (2006).
13. United States Department of Justice (1999).
14. United States Department of Justice (1999; 2004).
15. Deer (personal communication, 2003).

gests that this rate has changed. According to the United States Department of Justice in 1999[16] and again in 2004,[17] perpetrators of violence against Indigenous women are more likely to be of a different race, with a majority of acts committed by White men, although evidence is growing that cannot be ignored of violence by American Indian men against Indigenous women.

This evidence of the pervasive and disproportionate levels of VAAIW and the search for meaningful interventions targeting the multiple dynamics of oppression faced by First Nations women were the impetus for *Weaving Strength, Weaving Power*. The haunting issue for those engaged in research on violence against Indigenous women is determining not only the scope of the problem but identifying culturally meaningful strategies for healing and social change for ending this problem in the lives of tribal women. Obviously, the most definitive outcome for this problem is ending all violence and abuse against all women. This long-range strategy is inextricably linked to the intermediary transformation of conditions and social structures in society that promote domination and subjugation and requires social changes that focus on the structural dynamics of institutional oppression that support subjugation and oppression. More immediate outcomes include identifying effective strategies for ending violence against Indigenous women, as well as women generally. Approaches that emphasize resisting, rejecting, or neutralizing the negative effects of oppression are critical intermediaries towards long-term change to end violence and abuse against women and particularly those approaches that build upon the strengths within Indigenous women and cultures.

Exploring the phenomenon of VAAIW by examining the relationship between the experience of violence and the structural forces of colonialism that erode the power and place of women within First Nations has been the motivation for examining the various strands of oppression tribal women confront. Although such work is an important foundation for raising awareness or consciousness,

16. United States Department of Justice (1999).
17. United States Department of Justice & Perry (2004).

the next step—or the "So what?" question—requires application of the knowledge to ensure action is taken to produce the change needed. The framework for this work is based on assumptions of strength and the processes of engagement promoting self-determination in social action and social change to overcome the disempowerment produced by experiences of oppression.

Concepts related to empowerment from both Indigenous and mainstream social work perspectives were merged in the conceptualization of an empowerment framework for social change. This framework for _Indigenous empowerment_ emphasizes the inherent power situated in the cultures, systems, practices, and experiences of Indigenous Peoples, as well as the unique political status of Indigenous People as constitutionally sovereign and treaty-based Nations.[18] The work of Crow Creek Sioux scholar, Elizabeth Cook-Lynn rightly maintains the power of tribal peoples is located in this "indigenousness"—a primary source of empowerment for tribal peoples. By grounding empowerment in this concept of indigenousness, with the scholarship on strengths in the social work discipline, a culturally based conceptual framework is advanced, emerging from tribal communities and organizations. Empowerment scholarship counters messages of powerlessness evoked by violence-based oppression and engages women, in this case, in multiple levels of change promoting the eradication of violence in domains including the personal, interpersonal, community, and political domains.

By merging strengths and empowerment scholarship in social work with a theoretical framework responsive to the political, social, and cultural dynamics of Indigenous Nations that acknowledges the Indigenous colonization, an important contribution to the knowledge base of Indigenous Studies and Social Work is possible. By building on action-oriented frameworks for simultaneous

---

18. Cook-Lynn (2007, p. 116) describes the historic failure of European-based education, political, and legal systems to meet the needs of Indigenous Peoples and advances an "ethno-endogenous epistemological empowerment" model within the discipline of Indian Studies that recognizes and draws upon the inherent powers of Indigenous Peoples at multiple levels.

processes of change at multiple levels, including the individual, group, and community, cognizant of and committed to advancing the constitutionally sovereign and treaty-based status of tribal Nation, dual agendas for Indigenous empowerment are furthered. Consistent with both strengths and empowerment scholarship in social work, this approach builds on the strengths, resources, capacities, cultures, and experience of Indigenous Nations to challenge structures of privilege and oppression for the purpose of retaining and advancing political and cultural status as sovereign and treaty-based Nations. Building on existing empowerment frameworks, this culturally based model describes the mobilization of individuals, communities, and tribes toward social action and social change, based on tenets of indigenousness and sovereignty as advanced in the Indigenous Studies discipline.[19] It is important for tribal women oppressed by violence and abuse, and others oppressed by conditions of domination and oppression at multiple levels, to "take power back" on terms that honor the voice, strengths, and experiences of those impacted.

Indigenous empowerment frameworks are situated in the worldviews and philosophies of tribal cultures and linked to the systems and practices of these civilizations, including the strength, wisdom, and resiliency accrued from experience. These models are instrumental to those invested in the long-term capacity and sustainability of tribal Nations, while also contributing to the knowledge base for future generations. The effectiveness of social action and change is dependent on the strategies for mobilization and desire for social justice at many junctures. While this work occurs with, and by, those oppressed by undesirable conditions, as well as allies committed to the endeavor of creating a just society, empowerment is not something given to or done to "those people" but instead is the recognition of and access to inherent power and wisdom

---

19. This model proposes incorporating the work of leading social work scholars on strengths and empowerment, including Almeida (1993), Robbins, Chatterjee, & Canda (1998), Cox (1991), Cox & Stoltenberg (1991), Freeman (2001), GlenMaye (1998), Gutierrez & Ortega (1991), Parsons (1998), Saleebey (1997), and Weick & Saleebey (1995) with the work of Native Studies scholars such as Cook-Lynn (2007).

derived from centuries of resilience, coupled with meaningful access to resources and opportunities that promote capacity-building. Community activists, scholars, social workers, and social justice practitioners facilitate consciousness by tapping into inherent strengths, power, and resources while engaging processes of self-determination at multiple levels for social action and change.

*Weaving Power, Weaving Strength* is an important contribution to emerging scholarship for several reasons. First, it is clear Indigenous women are disproportionately affected by violence and abuse. Although this issue has garnered recent public attention, especially with the 2007 release of the Amnesty International *Maze of Injustice* report,[20] inadequate attention and resources have been focused on the structural dynamics of oppression that undergird practices of subjugation, such as violence against women. Too often, the grassroots strategies for social change and culturally based best practices for challenging violence against women are invisible in mainstream journals.

Second, the limited data on VAAIW, including prevalence and frequency data, obscure an understanding of the differences in the patterns and experiences of First Nations women and of the effects on those who have experienced violence and abuse compared with those who have not. Only recently has limited research begun to emerge on the prevalence and incidence of VAAIW; this research has primarily been centered in health-care settings serving tribal populations. The existing research is important, but also inadequate for designing effective intervention and responses for Indigenous women. Tribal governments need reliable data to develop policy, programs, and services sensitive to the needs of tribal women. The lack of information available to tribes affects the quality of decisions and hinders effective and multi-layered responses to the phenomenon of violence. The importance of the type of research undertaken is also examined using an exploratory quantitative study by an Indigenous scholar that examines the prevalence and incidence of violence against younger Indigenous women, as well as the differences on constructs associated with empowerment be-

---

20. Amnesty International (2007).

tween tribal women who have experienced violence and tribal women who have not.

Third, additional research is needed to strengthen the literature examining the contemporary implications of colonization on First Nations populations, including the relevance of Indigenous empowerment models that consider the historical effects of colonization in inducing structurally based violence and abuse against contemporary Indigenous women. Attention is focused on the structural dynamics of oppression faced by Indigenous People and the gendered impacts this experience has had on the attitudes, beliefs, behaviors, and practices toward women today. The destructive consequences of violence and abuse undermine and disrupt the traditional cultures of tribal peoples; this acknowledgement is essential to correct multiple levels of adopted dysfunction suffocating the traditional cultures of Indigenous Peoples.

Integrated critical analysis of the structural dynamics of oppression is proposed as a means for strategically identifying systemic change in Indigenous Nations. The use of multifocal examination of the overlapping intersections of culture, gender, class, and race in structures of oppression under conditions of colonialism promotes multi-layered change of the practices and systems that reinforce and promote subjugation of Indigenous women, which must be considered as strategies for change are identified. Colonization is alive and well and found in the adopted behaviors and values of colonization, social problems and conditions manifesting this reality, philosophies and worldviews of hierarchy and domination, and systems and structures antithetical to the traditional cultures of Indigenous Nations.

Colonization is found in unabated attacks by federal, state, and local governments on the rights of Indigenous governments to engage in the protection of homelands and natural resources. It is found in the ongoing erosion of sovereignty and self-determination exercised by Indigenous governments under siege by hostile court decisions. It is found in the ineptitude of federal bureaucracies charged with fulfilling treaty and trust obligations that abrogate fiduciary and ethical responsibilities in order to appease the anti-Indian agendas of special interest groups and multinational corporations intent on usurping the remaining rights and resources of tribes. It is also found within Indigenous communities who have succumbed to the forces of oppression by adopting the power structures of mainstream culture promoting domination and violence at the expense of tribal women and the Nation.

There is much to be understood about violence against women, beginning with the terms typically used in such discussions. The term *violence and abuse against women (VAAW)* is used to describe the pervasive and complex spectrum of violence experienced by women. This shift in terminology is inclusive of the physical, psychological, and emotional forms of abuse and trauma directed at women, as well as the social costs to those who have experienced violence and abuse. The term *violence and abuse* was recommended by practitioners, researchers, and other stakeholders to more accurately describe the continuum of violence and abuse experienced by women, and this term will be used here.[21] This term describes a range of VAAW, including physical, psychological, emotional, and sexual forms of trauma and abuse, as well as stalking and being threatened; the term has been used by this author in surveys of tribal women and their experiences of violence and abuse. Specific types of violence and abuse associated with VAAW include:

- *Physical victimization*—being slapped, hit, shoved, kicked, bitten, or knocked down;
- *Emotional abuse*—being putdown, yelled at, or made to feel inadequate;
- *Being threatened*—with a knife, gun, or other weapon;
- *Being stalked*—followed, spied on, sent unsolicited mail, received unsolicited phone calls, or left unwanted items; or
- *Sexual victimization*—being forced to have sex, sexually assaulted, raped, threatened with rape, or forcibly penetrated with fingers or objects.

---

21. United States Centers for Disease Control and Prevention (US CDC) (2000). A US CDC conference was instrumental in convening experts and advancing this terminology; the recommendations are referenced here.

The term *violence and abuse against Indigenous women (VAAIW)* is being advanced to describe the types of violence and abuse, as previously identified, which are also experienced by First Nations women.

In solidarity with First Nations scholars committed to decolonization, this author has chosen to use the terms *Indigenous* and *First Nations* interchangeably in this study, rather than the misnomers of *Indian, American Indian, Indians of North America,* or *Native American.* While these terms will be used in a limited manner, they are "counterfeit terms" that subjugate the rights of First Nations People to define their identity;[22] however, these are terms that remain embedded in the psyche of academic culture, library-cataloging systems, and in popular press.

---

22. I am particularly grateful to Dr. Michael Yellow Bird (Chair of Social Work Program, Humboldt University, Humboldt, CA [1994, 1998–2002]) for his scholarship on colonialism and models for decolonization, as well as for his influence and mentoring of emerging Indigenous social work and Indigenous Nations scholars throughout his academic career.

# Chapter Two

# Indigenous Oppression and Empowerment

*Prior to the arrival of the Western people, the Yup'ik were alone in their riverine and Bering Sea homeland — they and the spirit beings that made things the way they were. They were ruled by the customs, traditions and spiritual beliefs of their people, and shaped by these and their environment: the tundra, the river and the Bering Sea. Their world was complete; it was a very old world. They called it Yuuyaraq, "the way of being a human being" ... the Yup'ik world would go upside down; it would end* (Harold Napoleon, 1991, p. 4).

## The Roots of Indigenous Oppression

The colonization of the lands, the cultures, and the Indigenous People of North America is one of the most compelling examples of imperialism in the history of this nation, yet it is too often invisible, ignored, trivialized, or denied in much of the mainstream discourse about First Nations People. Indigenous scholars and others engaged in critical analysis of imperialism and the associated practices of colonialism have produced an impressive body of scholarship examining this history and the consequences of colonialism on Indigenous Peoples in the United States and globally.[1] This schol-

---

1. Blauner (1969); Brave Heart & DeBruyn (1998); Dobyns (1984); Sale (1990); Duran & Duran (1995); Alfred (1999); Yellow Bird (2000).

arship provides an important knowledge base and insight into the multiple and interlocking dynamics of oppression experienced by First Nations People and the patterns that continue today, important to a more complete understanding of Indigenous Nations.

Structural changes resulting from colonialism generated multiple layers of disruption in the traditional social organization and social systems of First Nations Peoples. Existing structures and practices considered inferior to European societies or subversive to the overall goals of colonialism were frequently targeted for elimination, including social systems of government, religion, education, family, economy, and an array of subsystems and practices that existed throughout the unique cultural civilizations of tribal peoples. Indigenous social structures and practices according value and status to women conflicted with European gender norms, thus providing presumed evidence of the inferiority of First Nations civilizations.[2] The imposition of structures and institutions reflecting European ideologies of "superiority" were imposed as civilized responses to the primitive savagery of Indigenous Peoples and became the preferred justification for the oppression of First Nations Peoples.[3] The imposition of organizations and systems valuing White male-based power hierarchies and ideologies of racial, gender, and class superiority, while simultaneously undermining and outlawing traditional Indigenous cultures and systems, produced massive disruption throughout the social organizations of Indigenous People and is currently manifested in multiple ways.[4] Today, many tribal communities, including Indian men, have been corrupted by attitudes and practices adopted from mainstream society that promote notions of male superiority, male dominance, and misogyny. Tribal people are not exempt from engaging in racist,

---

2. In the work of Klein & Ackerman (1995), Nagel (2003), and Sale (1990), the critique of structural disruption and the manipulation of perception to justify the heinous acts perpetrated against Indigenous Peoples is useful in understanding the effects on women and existing social organizations, including gendered systems and practices.

3. Bartky (1990); Nagel (2003); Sale (1990).

4. Bachman (1992); Blauner (1969).

homophobic, or misogynistic attitudes and practices or rejecting traditional cultural practices and knowledge of tribal peoples.

# The Matrix of Colonialism

Scholars from the fields of Social Work, Indigenous Studies, Law, Political Science, and a host of social science disciplines have generated an innovative body of scholarship over the past four decades dedicated to the examination of colonialism and its history of oppression. This literature is unique in its analysis of the multiple contexts and meaning of colonialism and in the culturally diverse and interdisciplinary perspectives on the topic. Such scholarship contributes to the foundation necessary for model building as the biological, psychological, social, cultural, spiritual, economic, political, and historical forces affecting the behavior, attitudes, and beliefs of First Nations People are considered.[5]

# Terminology: *Imperialism, Colonialism, Oppression, Colonization, Indigenous Decolonization,* and *Structural Frameworks*

*Imperialism* is commonly used to describe practices, attitudes, or theories endorsing the rights of a dominating culture to rule another culture. This sense of entitlement serves as the foundation for colonialism and is used as justification for subjugation and domination.[6]

---

5. Devens (1992); Robbins, Chatterjee, & Canda (1998); Yellow Bird & Chenault (1999).

6. Seminal work influencing the conceptualization of colonialism and imperialism for this chapter includes numerous scholars, particularly Blauner (1969), Gil (1998), GlenMaye (1998), Mullaly (1997), Said (1993), and Yellow Bird & Chenault (1999).

*Colonialism* describes the sustained series of events that are enacted by an invading power on another culture, which facilitates and perpetuates the development of a worldview and structures and social organization supporting an ideology of oppression. Central to such philosophies is an unequivocal sense of entitlement to engage in domination, exploitation, control, and oppression on the basis of presumed superiority. Both imperialism and colonialism are supported by a fundamental principle of superiority that has evolved over centuries. This superiority is defined by power relations promoting the unequivocal domination, exploitation, control, and oppression of one group, seen as inferior or different, by a group that views itself as superior to the oppressed group.

*Oppression* describes a condition of powerlessness that cuts across every system within a culture experienced at multiple levels. Ideologies associated with colonialism are perpetuated throughout the social institutions of the larger structure to justify actions and support systems of subjugation. The late Palestinian scholar, Edward Said, described *colonialism* as multidimensional and interlocking, with rippled layers of structural, physical, and psychological oppressions.[7] Strategies and solutions addressing fragments of these philosophies and practices are inadequate given the pervasive nature of this structural matrix of domination.

*Colonization*—or the *process phase of colonialism*—describes the ongoing means by which the oppression of people, cultures, and nations is accomplished and maintained. Socialization or assimilation into the new structure and the ideology of domination and superiority inherent to structures of oppression are transmitted through the social systems of that society, as people and cultures are hierarchically marginalized and socialized into powerlessness. Multiple levels of domination and exploitation ensure the maintenance of a matrix of structures, systems, policies, and practices justifying oppressive conditions, including discrimination, dehumanization, injustice, violence, and abuse. These structures solid-

---

7. Said (1978; 1993).

ify national and global systems of oppression, as well as an ideology of oppression throughout systems functioning within societies. Ongoing exposure to these processes of layered oppression produces a wide range of interpersonal and intrapersonal conflicts and trauma as those socialized and subjected to colonialism internalize negative images, worldviews, beliefs, and practices.[8]

*Indigenous decolonization* describes informed and willed strategies used at multiple levels and across Indigenous and mainstream systems by conscious First Nations People and allies to effect needed change and tribal-based solutions to pressing issues. Decolonization is facilitated through processes of reconnection to the strength of philosophies, knowledge, systems, and practices of First Nations, rather than a rejection of the Indigenous that comes with the adoption of colonial systems, processes, values, and knowledge. The intent is to address the multidimensional nature of colonialism, to mobilize efforts to revitalize, reclaim, and restore capacity, and to further advance the cultural viability of Indigenous Nations. These shifts are essential for the perpetuation of sovereignty, self-determination, and the protection of Indigenous homelands, cultures and resources for future generations as power is taken back.

*Structural frameworks* are advanced to ensure multidimensional analysis of issues such as violence and abuse against Indigenous women (VAAIW) in order to address the interplay between structural forces, systems, and social problems within society. A structural approach can enable understanding of the consequences of these dynamics in creating or contributing to existing social problems and can foster the creation of layered change strategies. In doing so, these frameworks facilitate movement away from the one-dimensional approaches of the past, particularly *deficit models* and *victim-blaming models,* and support movement toward multidimensional analysis. Structural frameworks introduce the potential for identifying and correcting multiple systemic root causes of conditions to ensure long-term change rather than short-term fixes.

---

8. Albert, Cagan, Chomsky, et al. (1986); Duran & Duran (1995); Mikaere (1999); Mullaly (1997).

The interplay between the oppression generated by colonialism and gender will be considered further by integrating the historical experiences of First Nations.

# Historical Context of Indigenous Colonization

Contact with the ideology of colonialism produced dramatic shifts in the worldviews and ideology of Indigenous Nations, which permeated the social structures and the socialization processes inherent to these systems. Events that produced extraordinary large-scale devastation, such as the overwhelming population declines, led to social disorganization affecting virtually every level of social structure and organization within Indigenous cultures. The demographic collapse caused by epidemics, warfare, and genocidal policies reduced First Nations from an estimated 5 to 12 million at the point of contact in 1492 with the Europeans to a point of near extinction by the early 1800s, when the population had declined to approximately 600,000.[9] Population declines occurred with the simultaneous enactment and enforcement of colonial, state, and federal policies supporting the removal and relocation of tribal peoples, the abolishment of tribal governments, and an assortment of oppressive tactics aimed at prohibiting the exercise of religious and cultural practices. Too often, however, consideration of structural forces such as demographic collapse is absent from analysis or these forces are treated as insignificant and unrelated factors.

Traditional spiritual, political, economic, and family systems promoting egalitarian and reciprocal structures within Indigenous Nations were systematically targeted for destruction, overthrown, collapsed, and replaced by more "civilized" models based on European patrilineal hierarchies.[10] Kinship and clan structures, edu-

---

9. Dobyns (1984); Sale (1990); Thornton (1987).

10. Perdue (1998) examines the effect of these practices on the Cherokee political structure and social organization; Gutierrez (1991) describes the disruption to Pueblo systems of organization in *When Jesus Came, the*

cation and cultural socialization processes, and gender roles and gendered systems at every level were disrupted and, in many cases, declared illegal.[11] Changes in gender roles changed the relationships between the sexes, the choices based on gender, and the value accorded an individual based on gender status and gendered systems within Indigenous societies. The decline in women's status and power followed changes in the traditional social structures and systems in which First Nations women assume significant roles and responsibilities.[12]

The ongoing nature of colonization, including the use of education systems and policies such as those related to boarding schools, emphasized indoctrination of First Nations People into the prevailing culture of oppression. The hierarchy of privilege introduced by the boarding school apparatus promoted the "superiority" of progressive and educated Indians over those who believed and followed the traditional ways. Hierarchies of intelligence based on gender and darkness of skin were used at boarding schools to determine the suitability of training and one's potential for success. It was believed that if Indigenous People were taught the superiority of Anglo cultures, they would return to the reservation to civilize [oppress] their own people.[13] The boarding school system was instrumental in molding young minds to gender- and race-specific notions of ability as defined by racist conceptions of First Nations People as an uncivilized and barbarian people. The consolidation of colonial rule in the United States was imposed uniformly and steadily reinforced by government-sponsored policies, including

---

*Corn Mothers Went Away;* and Mikaere (1999) describes the effects on Maori society. The shared patterns of this experience for Indigenous women globally are characteristic of colonialism.

11. Extensive scholarship by Indigenous women from multiple disciplines beginning in the 1970s documents this pattern and the effects on the roles of women and perceptions about tribal women. These scholars include Albers and Medicine (1983), Bataille & Sands (1984), Green (1975), and LaFromboise, Heyle, & Ozer (1990).

12. Albers & Medicine (1983); Klein & Ackerman (1995); LaFromboise, Heyle, & Ozer (1990).

13. Child (1998); LaFromboise, Heyle, & Ozer (1990); Trennert (1982).

the use of missionaries and mandatory education in boarding schools, systems designed to "domesticate and civilize" Indigenous women who were resistant to their new status as inferiors in male-dominated hierarchies.[14]

Tribal socialization practices—including the flexibility of gender role, the sexual freedom of these roles, and the matrilocal and the extended family patterns supporting Indigenous gender roles—were considered subversive to the colonial social order and thus required eradication. Controlling Indigenous women by eradicating the systems that upheld their rights and choices as well as reducing the power and status of women were both goals of colonization. The invading forces viewed the power of Indigenous women as an impediment to conquest and believed, rightly so, that "as long as women held unquestioned power of such magnitude, attempts at total conquest of the continents were bound to fail."[15] The gender wisdom of tribes is particularly poignant in recognizing the importance of the resistance of Indigenous women to the onslaught of structural forces encountered: *A nation is not defeated until the hearts of its women are on the ground.*

The reduction and collapse of the status, power, and gendered systems of Indigenous women was intended to weaken and destabilize First Nations and corresponded with the extension of colonial domination of Indigenous People in multiple arenas.[16] The pattern of abolishing spheres of influence and power for women and excluding the voice of women in the decision-making processes at every level meant that opposition to the changes being forced upon Indigenous Nations would no longer be heard. Indigenous male leadership that failed to cooperate in the disempowerment of women was routinely replaced with men selected on the basis of their willingness to engage in the oppression of women and the

---

14. The work of Child (1998), Devens (1992), Jaimes & Halsey (1992), and Lomawaima (1994) critically examine the effect of boarding schools on tribal women.

15. Gunn Allen (1992, p. 3).

16. Devens (1992); Jaimes & Halsey (1992); Klein & Ackerman (1995); Perdue (1980).

People.[17] These events set into motion what would become a long history of co-opting tribal leadership in order to advance agendas of imperialism and further disrupt the gendered social organization of tribes. In many cases, male-dominated political, religious, and social organizations were established within tribes to effectively subjugate Indigenous women by diminishing their rights, roles, power, and responsibilities.[18] The gendered prototype of colonization, as described by the Pueblo scholar Rámon Gutierrez,[19] is common in the patterns of colonialism across Indigenous Nations globally:

> *Conquest by a patriarchal society meant women lost to men their exclusive rights to land, to child labor, to seeds, and even to children ... Although all of the Puebloans were matrilineal at the time of the conquest, [those] in closest contact with Spanish towns became patrilineal or bilateral. Those Pueblos who most resisted Christianization — the Hopi, the Zuni, and the Keres at Acoma — remained matrilineal. Among these people we still find a vibrant array of women's fertility societies, spirited ceremonies to vivify the earth, and a host of descendant earthbound symbols that celebrate femininity* (Gutierrez, 1991, p. 79).

The disenfranchisement of Indigenous women began with the adoption of the "new" colonial social order, which marginalized the influence, power, and choice of women by imposing on tribes hierarchical systems controlled and ruled by men. The subordinate status of women inherent to these hierarchies contradicted the traditional cultural teachings found in the origin narratives and dis-

---

17. Perdue (1980) describes the effects of the imposition of male-dominated political systems on the Beloved Women Society of the Cherokee. Numerous historians discuss the effects of these changes on gendered systems and on male-female relationships.

18. Anderson (1985); Gutierrez & Ortega (1991); LaFromboise, Berman, & Sohi (1994); LaFromboise, Heyle, & Ozer (1990); Livingston (1974).

19. Gutierrez (1991).

rupted the gendered systems and egalitarian practices within Indigenous Nations. These practices continue to be viewed as the source of distrust and antagonism between Indigenous women and tribal men, especially in those communities that adopted misogynist practices towards women. As the traditional forms of First Nations social structures and governments were centralized, social, political, and economic power increasingly rested in the hands of a few elite men who adopted the Anglo-defined tenets of civilization, lured by the promise of individual gain over the interests of the People.[20] The contamination of egalitarian systems and the corrosive effects of these hierarchical practices are evident in tribal communities that were once rich with gendered systems and ceremonies but that no longer retain practices and ceremonies honoring women or recognize the significance of gender, including puberty ceremonies for males and females. It is not uncommon, for example, for tribes today to identify as patriarchies, when in fact, the emergence narratives, origin stories, and oral histories describe times and practices in which matriarchies and matrilineal systems were the norm. Systems and practices predicated on notions of balanced reciprocity were routinely targeted, although the success in fully abolishing these systems varies. Conscious efforts were made in many tribes to take traditional practices "underground" in order to ensure the survival of the Indigenous cultures and practices, including gendered practices and systems. The significant shifts in the privilege and influence given to men as a result of the wholesale transfer of power served to strengthen the benefits of male-dominated hierarchical systems, to disrupt traditional cultures, and to reinforce the subjugation of Indigenous women and Nations by turning the world upside down.[21]

---

20. Perdue (1980; 1998); Shepardson (1995).

21. As previously noted, Napoleon (1991) describes righting an Indigenous world turned "upside down" (p. 4).

# Caricatures, Stereotypes, and Invisibility of the Contemporary Indigenous Women

The belief that Indigenous women had little power and were forever subject to a life of domination and exploitation has been perpetuated in stereotypes and by omission and misrepresentation in popular and scholarly literature.[22] These practices serve the function of upholding the superiority of Anglo gender roles and beliefs while portraying Indian life as morally and culturally inferior and undesirable.[23] Absent from a world of scholarship historically controlled and authored by White men are histories of Indigenous cultures that accurately interpret the roles, status, power, and influence of tribal women. Instead, disparaging portrayals of Indigenous women are mired in constructed images advanced in cowboy movies, cartoons, and stereotypes that continue to serve as the basis for informing and shaping public opinion. The extent to which these representations inform in the 21st century is nonetheless astounding, particularly when professionals who are among the best educated and, seemingly, socially conscious representatives of progressive disciplines, have not been challenged to critically examine these constructed representations.

Among the most damaging of the stereotypes faced by First Nations women are those related to sexualized stereotypes. Stereotypes and representations depicting Indigenous women as promiscuous are very old tactics of imperialism, used to control women and to justify heinous atrocities, including misogynistic torture against women throughout the world. These gendered distortions have been perpetuated in a wide body of literature and historical narratives since contact occurred between First Nations People and the invading forces of Europe. Gender propaganda continues to be used today in military campaigns of genocide that seek

---

22. Albers & Medicine (1983).
23. Nagel (2003).

to demonize women in order to destroy cultures. The torture of women, including rape and the sexual mutilation of genitalia occurring in Rwanda, for example, is not unlike that to which Indigenous women in the America's were subjected at the hands of colonial forces over the past 500 years. Sexualized images have been consistently used to disparage Indigenous women and as justification for coerced sexual exchanges involving rape, forced prostitution, and sexual slavery at the hands of invaders, as well as a wide range of VAAIW.[24] The extent to which gender-specific stereotypes continue to operate in the psyche of American men is unknown; however, these representations are continually used to degrade and marginalize tribal women as well as used in the marketing of violence against tribal women.

Andrea Smith, activist and scholar of Cherokee descent, has written extensively about the use of sexual violence as a tool of colonialism and oppression that is intended to subjugate women. The lack of regard for tribal Nations and the bodies of Indigenous women make them "sexually violable"—raping bodies that are inherently impure does not count, nor does the history of mutilation of Indian bodies, both living and dead.[25] As Smith points out, the dehumanization of Indigenous women did not end in 1492 but continues in modern day, as reflected in the 1982 release of an adult video game *Custer's Revenge*[26] in which players score points for raping an Indian women, in ongoing sexual violence, and in trafficking of Indigenous women globally.

In 2008, several radio stations in Washington State, North Carolina, and Alaska used the airwaves to broadcast disturbingly racist and sexist programming segments by radio shock jocks spouting anti-Indian tirades attacking Indigenous women. On an Alaska radio station (100.5 "The Fox"[27]), two disc jockeys—Woody and Wilcox—joked that "[you are not an Alaskan until you have] made love to

---

24. Hurtado (1997); Nagel (2003).
25. Smith (2005).
26. Classic Gaming (2008); Mystique/PlayAround (1982); Video Game Critic (2008).
27. Clear Channel Communications, Inc. (2010).

the Yukon River and peed in a Native woman."[28] There was no out-
cry from then Alaska State Governor Sarah Palin or demands for apology from her on behalf of Indigenous women in Alaska. In
Washington State, tribal women were referred to as "drunks and
'hoes'" on public airwaves without outrage from mainstream lis-
teners. After a grassroots mobilization of Indigenous People by
Roxanne Chinook (an activist who works to end violence against
Native American Indian women), the radio stations were threatened with the loss of significant tribal advertising campaigns in
Washington State and inundated with nationwide condemnations.[29]
It was not until advertising revenues were threatened that a problem was acknowledged. While apologies were eventually and re-
luctantly extended and airtime was given to the topic of violence
against Indian women, these patterns of institutionalized and racist
misogyny abound, too often times without redress. It should be
noted states in the Northwest have been at the epicenter of legal
battles by Indigenous Nations to protect treating and fishing rights
and this region is increasingly identified as hot spots for White extremist groups. These incidents are similar in the lack of outrage
from average citizens by these "harmless" acts and too often dismissed.

We are reminded by Tutsi scholar Llezlie Green that the use of
radio, cartoons, newspapers, and literature by extremist Hutu pro-
pagandists fueled the hatred of the Tutsi, and especially Tutsi women
and their sexuality, which resulted in seemingly unimaginable and
horrific sexual violence against women. Green noted this campaign
was intended as a "step in the process of deconstruction of the Tutsi

---

28. Julie Kitka, President of the Alaska Federation of Natives (Anchorage, AK), notes, "On April 9, [2008], one of the radio personalities
on the 'Woody and Wilcox' show on KBFX 100.5-FM, made brutally of-
fensive racial remarks on the morning show. The two were bantering about
what it means to be a real Alaskan. One asked the question "Have you ever
made love to the Yukon River or peed in a Native woman?" (Kitka, 2008).

29. Roxanne Chinook, activist to end violence against Native American Indian women (personal communication, October 29, 2008 [e-mail
apology letter from KUBE 93.3 FM, Seattle, WA]).

group—destruction of the spirit, of the will to live, and of life it-self" in her writing, *Sexual Violence Against Tutsi Women in Rwanda in 1994*.[30] The torture and brutalization of women has been continually used as a tactic in the genocide of cultures in nations founded on or corrupted by principles of oppression and misogyny.[31] The sexual torture and genocide against Tutsi women is not unlike that experienced by Indigenous women by colonial forces.

In 1999, a report by the United States Department of Justice found that Indigenous women are raped at a rate more than double that of rapes reported by all races;[32] little has changed a decade later.[33] In addition, First Nations women who are raped most often reported that the victimization involved an offender of a different race. In 1999, it was reported that at least 70% of violent victimization experienced by First Nations People is committed by persons of a different race (non-First Nations), a substantially higher rate of interracial violence than experienced by White or Black women.[34] In 2002, this rate had declined to 60% according to the most recent Department of Justice report on American Indians and Crimes.[35] The effect of stereotypes, invisibility, and ongoing exposure to these elements of oppression on contemporary First Nations women has not been examined in disciplines such as Social Work and Indigenous Studies, but clearly a social problem exists with the potential for a range of interpersonal and intrapersonal conflict and trauma.

The many grassroots voices speaking on issues of colonization and oppression recognize the complex relationship between social problems and colonization at multiple levels. Advocating for critical education about the roots of contemporary social problems in Indigenous communities, these approaches serve to raise consciousness and mobilize communities for change that addresses the

---

30. Green (n.d.).
31. Green (1975).
32. United States Department of Justice (1999).
33. United States Department of Justice & Perry (2004).
34. United States Department of Justice (1999).
35. United States Department of Justice & Perry (2004).

effects of colonization in the lives of Indigenous People. Tribally based programs are one such initiative, such as Cangleska, Inc. (Kyle, SD), a Lakota-based community intervention program. The impact of colonization on gender systems is reflected in workshops and educational literature disseminated by Cangleska based on Lakota culture and experiences. These community-based approaches promote taking power back by using cultural wisdom, experience, and teachings while acknowledging the original source of violence against Indian women:

> *In pre-reservation tribal society, women held status and were honored and respected for their roles as life givers and nurturers. With colonization Indian women were defined by Western mainstream standards that reflect the belief of our colonizers ... The post-colonization status of native women renders them just as vulnerable to abuse as any other race of women. The result of this history of oppression is confusion about proper behavior, i.e., violence against Oglala women* (Cangleska, Inc., 2000, pp. 4–5).

Although practices inherent to colonization and oppression disrupted—and, in many cases, obliterated—egalitarian systems, the concept of women's rights, gender issues, and feminism have frequently been rejected by contemporary First Nations women who retain cultural practices and systems reflective of balanced reciprocity. These systems are defined by the recognition of differences in the roles of men and women, with neither gender being viewed as superior. In systems of reciprocity, all genders are essential for the well-being or balance of a society,[36] including third genders or 'two-spirited' people; however, these gender systems were also targeted, abolished, or banished during 'civilization' campaigns.

It should come as no surprise that, as hierarchical systems were adopted, the social costs to Indigenous women have been high. Gender-based critiques of the multiple levels of structural disrup-

---

36. Henrietta Mann, eminent Cheyenne scholar, (personal communication, 1993); Klein & Ackerman (1995).

tion accompanying the experience of colonization and oppression in First Nations communities and the magnitude of these changes on the roles and treatment of women can no longer be unilaterally dismissed or ignored. Maori scholar, Linda Tuhiwai Smith acknowledges the pervasive impacts of gender disruption in every sphere of life, including the social structure of Maori Nations:

> *Family organization, child rearing, political and spiritual life, work and social activities were all disordered by a colonial system which positioned its own women as the property of men with roles which were primarily domestic. Indigenous women across many different societies claim an entirely different relationship, one embedded in the beliefs about the land and the universe, about the spiritual significance of women and about the collective endeavors that were required in the organization of society* (Smith, 1999, p. 151).

The oppression of traditional ideologies, the elimination of structures and worldview that support women and the effects of colonization are strikingly similar whether considering the Pueblo of the Southwest, the Ojibwa of the Great Lakes, the Cherokee of the Carolinas, the Hawaiians of the South Pacific, or the Maori of New Zealand. Emerging Mohawk scholar and grassroots activist Jessica Yee[37] describes the impact of colonization on reproductive health and the choices of Indigenous women:

> *Many of the values, practices, and traditions once held strong in our Aboriginal communities are now lost, and this most definitely includes the rightful place of our women to govern their own bodies. For many nations, reproductive health issues were decisions made by the individual, and were not thrust into the political arena for any kind of public scrutiny. The core decision-making for Indigenous women takes place between her and the Great Spirit or Creator, whoever that may be for her. With the impo-*

---

37. Yee (2009).

*sition of colonization and Christianity, which brought in cultural genocide and systemic assimilation, conflicting belief systems were forced upon our people to an extreme extent* (Yee, 2009, paragraph 8).

The effects of colonialism and the subsequent oppression of traditional ideologies as well as the elimination of gendered systems and worldviews valuing women among Indigenous women are too often a shared global pattern and experience of Indigenous women. The effects of a conflict in values on the Indigenous women of Aotearoa (New Zealand) is described by Jenkins in the analysis of patriarchy by Mikaere and her recognition of the colonial processes affecting Indigenous women globally:[38]

*Western civilization when it arrived on Aotearoa's shores, did not allow its womenfolk any power at all — they were merely chattel in some cases less worthy than the men's horses. What the colonizer found was a land of noble savages narrating, stories of the wonder of women. Their myths and beliefs had to be reshaped and retold. The missionaries were hell bent (heaven-bent) on destroying their pagan ways. Hence, in the retelling of our myths, by Maori male informants to Pakeha male writers who lacked the understanding and significance of the Maori cultural beliefs, Maori women find their* mana wahine *[sacredness] destroyed*[39] (Jenkins, 1988, p. 161).

# Indigenous Social Work

Research examining the manifestations of colonization in the lives of contemporary Indigenous women has been examined by Indigenous social work scholars. Lowery examines the relationship between addictions and the experiences of First Nations women,[40]

---

38. Mikaere (1999).
39. Jenkins (1988).
40. Lowery (1998).

who have borne the brunt of disenfranchising practices inherent to colonization. Although focused on the specific issue of addiction, Lowery views colonization as a trigger for a loss of meaning and further views addictions as a manifestation of this disruption. Brave Heart and DeBruyn advanced the concept of historical unresolved grief created from the experience of colonization and developed surveys to document grief experiences among the Lakota.[41] Again, the relationship between colonization and the grief experiences of contemporary Lakota Peoples is central to the analysis. These early groundbreaking studies forced examination of the effects of colonization on Indigenous women and challenged the notion that Indigenous experiences of colonization had no consequences or relationship to social problems experienced in these communities today.

# Allies in Collaboration with First Nations

Disciplines and practitioners sensitive to the dynamics of cultural diversity, who are conscious of the dynamics of oppression and prepared to work collaboratively with First Nations are important allies in social change and action within Indigenous Nations. Those committed to the social justice agendas of First Nations are documenting the structural disruption across systems; developing decolonization strategies for overcoming and healing the oppressive legacy of colonization; and working to build capacity within Indigenous communities. This work of social action, social change, and community organization cannot occur without knowledge of First Nations People and the Indigenous experience of colonialism or an understanding of the importance of sovereignty and self-determination. The ability to engage in critical and multidimensional self-reflection about the role of structural forces in the oppression of Indigenous Nations and a willingness to consider the relationship of these experiences to social conditions today is an impor-

---

41. Brave Heart & DeBruyn (1998).

tant shift away from victim-blaming approaches of the past. On-going evaluation of the role of various academic disciplines in hin-dering self-determination and facilitating the subjugation of Indigenous Nations, including social work, must be reconciled. Such preparation may prepare a new generation of professionals to collaborate with, advocate for, and facilitate the work of grass-roots activists and practitioners who have the expertise needed in the development and implementation of culturally based healing mod-els and strategies, based upon strengths found in the traditional Indigenous social structures and practices that may prove to be more responsive to the multiple levels of disruption that have oc-curred. Processes such as those described may contribute to the advancement of decolonization and the empowerment of Indige-nous Peoples, but only when talking honestly about the truth is promoted and not punished.

# Recapturing Power by a Strengths-Based Empowerment Model

A strengths-based empowerment framework integrating litera-ture from the social work discipline on strengths and empower-ment is useful for addressing the structural dynamics of Indigenous oppression. This framework is consistent with the cultural world-views and philosophies of Indigenous Peoples as well as the work of decolonization and social justice within tribal communities that recognize their own existing strengths and resources. *Empower-ment* describes the simultaneous processes of change—or taking power back—required at multiple levels, resulting from disrup-tive structural conditions or forces, affecting individuals, groups, communities, Indigenous Nations, and others.[42] Given the multi-dimensional nature of colonialism, approaches cognizant of struc-

---

42. This work draws from the scholarship of scholars of color, in-cluding Gutierrez & Ortega (1991), Gutierrez, Parsons, & Cox (1998), and GlenMaye (1998).

tural disruption and strategies promoting structural and layered change ensure a theoretical fit for analysis and work. Empowerment frameworks are incomplete without incorporation of social action strategies, practice, and processes to challenge and change structures of privilege and oppression. A large body of literature on strengths within the social work discipline emphasizing the utilization of the strengths and resources within individuals, groups, and communities complement the emphasis of empowerment on mobilizing capacity to generate social action and social change. These related strands of work are equally important with disenfranchised communities, but also important in signifying a shift away from deficit analysis. Theoretical frameworks based on empowerment and strengths concepts provide a mechanism for addressing significant structural and social disruption, using the experience, political status, and indigenousness of tribal peoples, or the strengths, resources, and capacity of Indigenous Nations to create and sustain momentum toward lasting change.

A steady stream of academic scholarship on empowerment over the past 25 years has provided the necessary foundation for exploratory studies that examine the usefulness of empowerment practice in multiple settings. Early work suggests there are at least three levels of change that occur as power is taken back, including the personal, interpersonal, and community/political spheres of empowerment.[43] To fully realize and utilize one's inherent power, shifts must occur in each domain promoting awareness of an array of structural and situational factors that influence self-perception and attitudes (*personal* sphere); knowledge and skills (*interpersonal* sphere) and actions and behaviors (*community/political* sphere). As individuals take power back, these changes produce ripple effects on related systems, including family, community, and nation. These domains were used in the 2004 exploratory study on the prevalence and incidence of violence and abuse in a sample of tribal college women,[44] and served as well as the basis for an empowerment frame-

---

43. Gutierrez & Ortega (1991); Parsons (1998).
44. Chenault (2004).

work used in the review of empirical research from 1977 to 2000,[45] both of which are discussed later in text.

Empowerment frameworks challenge a sole focus on personal and interpersonal deficiencies because such approaches reinforce blaming victims for conditions of powerlessness. Instead, empowerment practice and approaches shift attention to include the analysis of policies and power dynamics that support oppression and perpetuate inequity—but the work does not stop there. These approaches are intended to promote engagement in community and/or political action to change or end the source of oppressive social conditions as a means towards realizing social justice—without this element, empowerment is limited. Given the emphasis on structural dynamics and the commitment to social change, empowerment frameworks are well suited for addressing an array of issues faced by Indigenous Nations, including VAAIW. The broad outcomes identified across the empirical literature on violence and abuse were categorized using an empowerment framework and appear in **Table 2.1**. This Table identifies the statistically significant out-

### Table 2.1 Mainstream Empowerment-Based Outcomes

| Personal Empowerment | Interpersonal Empowerment | Community/Political Empowerment |
| --- | --- | --- |
| Self-perception and attitudes | Knowledge and skills | Actions and behaviors |
| Self-esteem* Feelings of depression Anxiety level Stress level Self-efficacy* Attitude toward marriage and family Attitude toward feminism | Appraisal/Social support* Assertiveness Communication skills Problem-solving skills Sense of belonging Ability to access and use resources | *— none —* |

* Statistically significant outcomes.

---

45. Robbins, Chatterjee, & Canda (1998).

comes identified in the intervention research, which include self-esteem, self-efficacy, and appraisal support.

# Colonization and Empowerment

If one accepts the premise of Edward Said, the late Palestinian scholar, as it relates to the multidimensionality of colonialism,[46] it is evident multiple levels of social change are simultaneously required throughout the existing social structures and organizations, within both Indigenous and mainstream systems. A key tenet of social work and Indigenous Studies is framed by a commitment to social justice and social change as discussed previously. There is much work to be done throughout the larger social structure and the many social systems operating within society.

Numerous studies have been undertaken examining the relationship of empowerment to improved functioning; however, no empirical studies using an empowerment framework have been used to document the social problems facing Indigenous People, including the issue of VAAIW or the experience of Indigenous colonization and oppression. The literature on empowerment in social work, like that found in the practice research, tends to emphasize transformation of perceptions, beliefs, and behaviors at the personal and interpersonal levels, to the neglect of structural or environmental conditions or social action in these arenas.[47] Empowerment and social justice clearly require this third dimension if inequality and oppression are targets of change and if victim-blaming or deficit approaches of the past are to be overcome. While Indigenous Peoples are resilient and have unique strengths and resources derived from experiences and traditional cultures, an emphasis on strengths alone will not produce strategic social action to overcome the structural dynamics of oppression and, in this case, to end VAAIW.

---

46. Said (1978; 1993).
47. Rappaport (1997).

Instead, analysis of the ideological and structural dynamics of colonialism, the utilization of Indigenous resilience, and ongoing social change at multiple levels is essential to decolonization, social justice, and Indigenous empowerment. Examination of the systemic and broad changes that fundamentally altered the worldviews, social structures, and social organizations of First Nations provide a necessary foundation for understanding the historical forces that affected gender roles, as well as the civilizations of Indigenous Nations. While some Indigenous Nations were successful in resisting the forces of colonization, others were forced to adopt imposed systems or change in order to survive, which created an asymmetry of experiences related to the effects of colonization, including the effects on gendered systems, roles, and status of First Nations women within these cultures. Indigenous women whose status and power remained relatively intact, whose tribes were geographically remote and less accessible, who retained systems of social support—such as gender reciprocity or gendered systems and ceremonies—or culturally meaningful kinship and clan systems for dealing with changes that were occurring, likely had a very different experience of colonization and oppression that those who did not benefit from the protective factor of such experiences.[48]

Consciousness of the multiple dynamics of oppression supported by ideologies of colonialism is central to the empowerment of those living with such conditions, particularly when critically engaging inconsistency between the way things are now and the life instructions found within traditional systems of knowledge. Too often, stereotypes and distortions become the false images emulated by young tribal people, disenfranchised by histories of despair, defeat, and invisibility, inculcated through education and media and throughout mainstream society. Approaches used by Indigenous activists, community organizers, and scholars challenge institutionalized knowledge based upon deficit orientations and advance scholarship and research critiquing the gaps and flawed premises of

---

48. Jacobs (1995); Klein & Ackerman (1995); Tohe (2000).

disciplinary knowledge and approaches throughout the academy. Those working for social change emphasize the importance of mobilizing energy, critical consciousness, resources, and commitment in order to confront, challenge, and change the unidimensional oppressions encountered by marginalized groups and oppressed people, as discussed by Fowlkes.[49] Consciousness-raising activities and practices that give voice to the reality and experiences of women reduce shame and self-blame while working toward change of self and society.

Empowerment approaches promoting the engagement of women in social change are often reflected in the culturally based approaches used in tribal settings. The emphasis of tribal programs often addresses all three dimensions of empowerment (personal, interpersonal, and community/political spheres). However, these programs are equally distinct in the methods used to facilitate taking power back.

Engagement in social action within tribal programs occurs earlier in the process and often uses culturally based activities, practices, and ceremonies that reinforce the value of women within traditional cultures and examining the effect of colonialism on disrupting these systems. Using community education, political activism, and advocacy, women in these programs often engage in campaigns much earlier in the healing process to end violence against Indigenous women and to challenge the systems within tribal communities that ignore this problem, including the political and cultural systems. Cecilia Fire Thunder described processes in Lakota communities in which tribal women organized "Get Out the Vote" campaigns based on candidate responses to questions about violence against tribal women. Candidates were asked, "If elected, will you provide leadership that will not tolerate violence against women and will you pledge that you will not engage in violence against your wife, your children or any other women?" Candidates who refused to respond were not voted for.[50]

---

49. Fowlkes (1997).
50. Fire Thunder (2000).

In these same communities, a tribally operated community radio station is used to broadcast radio shows devoted to the topic of violence against Indian women. Women engaged in community education were joined by tribal men who had engaged in violence but participated in culturally based programs for male batterers. These Lakota men challenged the notion that violence against women is a "women's issue." Advocating for change in men's behavior and using themselves as examples, these men encouraged other men to stand with women in confronting this issue. It is not unusual in tribal communities committed to nation-building, to have resocialization programs for men that incorporate traditional cultural beliefs and knowledge to ensure that the male dynamics of violence are addressed in the healing strategies required to overcome this legacy of colonization.

The emphasis on community action in tribal communities likely produces multiple changes and benefits to individual, interpersonal, and community empowerment. The literature on the dynamics of violence and abuse often discusses the social isolation and estrangement in interpersonal relationships produced by violence, with a focus on improving self-esteem using individual and group counseling. Tribal approaches restore self-esteem and a sense of belonging by engaging women in social change or service to others. Engagement in community or political action becomes the mechanism for reconnecting women to healthy support systems in communities in a less intrusive and pathological manner. It is normal for women in tribal settings to be socially or politically active and such participation does not require being labeled as a *victim* or *survivor*, but instead a *member of the community*. These opportunities for engagement expand the knowledge and skills about violence and abuse; enable helping others by engaging in social change activities; reconnect individuals in communities with the support networks and resources needed; and mobilize individuals and communities to build and strengthen capacity. Empowerment is not an isolated or fragmented experience, but instead a phenomenon that is both integrated and related to both internal and external processes and interactions. Elements of this preliminary model of Indigenous empowerment are found in **Table 2.2**. Such approaches are often reflected in spiritually and culturally based approaches used in tribal communities but remain conspicuously absent in the literature.

Table 2.2  Indigenous Empowerment-Based Outcomes

| Personal Empowerment | Interpersonal Empowerment | Community/Political Empowerment |
|---|---|---|
| Self-perception and attitudes | Knowledge and skills | Actions and behaviors |
| Pride<br>Dignity<br>Reduction of shame<br>Strengths as a woman | Consciousness-raising<br>Critical thinking<br>Sense of belonging<br>Social support<br>Knowledge and skills | Revitalization of gender and natural support systems and activities<br>Revitalization of tribal healing practices and women's ceremonies<br>Community education<br>Activism and advocacy |

# Chapter Three

# Indigenous Feminism: Roots and Contemporary Expression

*In the 1970s, my grandmother was approached by white feminists "organizing" on our reservation and asked whether she would attend a bra-burning protest by her visitors. Her response ... we never let them put those things on us in the first place. I was raised and influenced by strong, independent and culturally grounded tribal women and men who provided my cultural grounding and helped me to understand what it means to be a* Bodewadmi quah. *I was politicized by the Red Power movement, inspired by the activism of grassroots scholars and practitioners, and enlightened by the scholarship of Indigenous academics* (Ahquapko, 2009, personal communication).

Indigenous feminism has been long centered in the cultures, systems, and practices of First Nations Peoples and can be found in countless tribal narratives of strong and fiercely independent Indigenous women who have been at the forefront of resistance to colonization, oppression, and change. Concerned with the survival and viability of First Nations, it has often been the responsibility of women to remind the People of the cultural traditions and philosophies that define Indigenous People, to challenge the disconnect between these cultural traditions and philosophies and circumstances, and to advocate for change in the conditions and problems arising from these circumstances at given points throughout history.

While much of the impetus for formal scholarship on gender developed from the Women's Movement in the 1960s, mainstream feminist theory has been successful in forcing examination of the multiple ways women have been and continued to be oppressed and marginalized and has called for action in creating social change. Gender research produced significant shifts in attitudes and changes in policies and social conditions, as well as change within social institutions reflecting a commitment to the empowerment of women—but it would be foolish to believe this work is done. New and diverse generations of feminists of color, whose realities and views are affected by different vantage points and conditions in the hierarchy of oppression, have joined in a collective effort and movement for change to challenge structures of oppression. The incorporation of marginalized voices in theory development, scholarship, and research strategies is fundamentally shifting the examination and approaches across disciplines. Increasingly, feminist analysis is forcing examination of the multiple ways women are oppressed and marginalized and has reinvigorated the call for action within communities of culture and of color, cognizant of the multiple oppressions faced by women of culture and color.

The recognition and use of strategies and approaches conscious of the structural conditions that perpetuate subjugation is a mainstay in much of the work of decolonization occurring within First Nations, equally relevant to gender research and Indigenous feminism. Indigenous women have historically been actively engaged in movements to protect and advance sovereignty and self-determination as the inherent rights and political status of First Nations because these powers theoretically protect the cultures of tribal peoples, including gendered systems and the power of Indigenous women. Long-standing cultural traditions have been instrumental in preparing and supporting Indigenous women to assert their power and use their influence by speaking on issues of importance. Across tribes, women have been and continue to be at the forefront of resistance campaigns opposing efforts designed to erode or terminate the sovereign rights of tribes in a host of social, political, environmental, cultural, and legal arenas. Multiple generations of women, experienced in sociocultural activism, are frequently among the strongest advocates of a traditionally based Indigenous feminism that has evolved over centuries from the worldviews, philosophies, cultures, history, status, and experiences of Indigenous Nations. Not content with waiting for academic studies to define problems for them or federally funded programs to prioritize pressing issues, tribal women have a long history of advocacy and engagement in campaigns for culturally based social and political change.

# Indigenous Feminism and Intersectionality

Contemporary Indigenous feminism is notable for its incorporation of emphasis on the structural dynamics of oppression, particularly the imposition and entrenchment of patriarchal hierarchies and both historic and continued efforts to disenfranchise and erode the power of tribal women. Indigenous feminism speaks to the "intersectionality" of oppression and subordination as described by Crenshaw and others,[1] while advancing the concept to describe the use of violence and abuse against Indigenous women (VAAIW) as a tool of colonialism and racism. Indigenous women, subjected to the interlocking dynamics of oppression on the basis of political status, culture, race, gender, social class, and sexual orientation, within both tribal and non-tribal settings, have no interest in replicating hierarchies of power and privilege in which the priorities, agendas, and rights of tribal women are diminished. This structural difference in orientation has caused many Indigenous women globally to reject mainstream feminism as irrelevant to the capacity- and nation-building efforts of Indigenous Nations, particularly when solutions are based upon upholding and perpetuating hierarchical systems of power.

The long history and practices emanating from imperialism have consistently subjugated the cultures and gendered systems of In-

---

1. Crenshaw (1991); Smith (2005).

digenous Nations, while elevating hierarchical systems and practices that privilege the knowledge and practices of the oppressors of tribal peoples. Indigenous feminist analyses consider the powerful dynamics inherent to systems of oppression, including the rewards gained by those willing to uphold the hierarchical status quo and the allure of the status and power acquired in such systems. Women who have benefitted from class, ethnicity, the benefit of education and resources, privilege, and proximity to male power brokers are not immune to engaging in domination, as found in the active participation of women in the oppression of women marginalized by practices of subjugation, including Indigenous Nations.[2] This internalization of oppression ensures the perpetuation of systems of domination by the hierarchical power structure as discussed by Freire.[3] First Nations Peoples have been affected by these dynamics as well. Some of the scholarship on the Red Power Movement explores the tension produced by male leadership that devalued the important contributions of Indigenous women. The incongruence between the disrespectful treatment of women and the traditional cultural practices by men in the American Indian Movement eventually eroded support among traditional grassroots organizers, activists, and supporters in many tribal communities and allies from the larger sociopolitical movement. It should be understood efforts to monopolize the pressing agendas of Indigenous Peoples that exclude the voices of disenfranchised women in decision-making processes or seek to replicate imposed powerlessness in hierarchical structures are irrelevant to First Nations globally, no matter who the perpetrators of oppression are. The fierce resistance to and rejection of structural forces of oppression, including male and female dominated hierarchies, is a commitment to self-survival, as well as to the cultural and political survival of sovereign Indigenous Nations.

---

2. Tadiar (1993).
3. Freire (1970; 1998).

# Violence against Indigenous
# Women Is Not Traditional

The power and place of tribal women is centered in and reinforced by the strength of unique traditional cultural teachings, knowledge, and wisdom about gender within Indigenous Nations. In these systems, both males and females have significant roles in maintaining the overall systems that serve as foundations for community, including gender systems. In these systems, the community has the imperative to observe and correct behaviors and practices inconsistent with the cultures in order to ensure survival, including behaviors that devalue women. Rejection of the inherent worldviews and values associated with these traditional teachings is found in behavior such as VAAIW and community behaviors that accept, deny, or normalize culturally dysfunctional conduct. Behavior, attitudes, and practices that promote domination, devaluation, and disrespect for First Nations women diminish the centrality of women within tribal society; weaken family and gender systems within Indigenous cultures; divert energy, time, and resources; and threaten the viability and sustainability of cultures.

The absence of vibrant, strong, healthy, and independent Indigenous women throughout the systems of Indigenous Nations—whether these roles are assumed in raising children, in advocacy for the People, or within the traditional practices and ceremonies of First Nations or leadership—ensure the extinction of cultures that must be lived in order to survive. Embedded throughout the teachings of Indigenous cultures are lessons focusing on the resiliency, resourcefulness, and capacity of women and the vital importance of the many roles and contributions of women to the survival of the People. These traditions, these ways of life, provide an important baseline from which to critique the contradictions in worldviews and ideologies related to gender that have resulted from colonialism-induced disruption seen today in behavior such as VAAIW. Such approaches are echoed in the consciousness-raising mantra introduced by the Lakota, now adopted by numerous tribes and resonating throughout the United States and Canada, "Violence against Indian women is not [Lakota] tradition."[4]

# Centrality of Women within Indigenous Cultures

Challenging the normalization of dysfunctional gender conduct, such as violence against women, cannot be isolated from examination of the adoption of misogynistic systems and ideologies that have contaminated practices and beliefs about women within tribal and mainstream communities. Nor can this work be disconnected from the corrosive effects of colonialism on Indigenous cultures and Nations. The centrality of women within Indigenous cultures and the emphasis on teachings that accord a value for the status of and the respect given to women is woven throughout the cultures of tribal people. A culture or nation without the contributions, voice, passion, strength, and guidance of women is defeated. The strengthening and revitalization of cultural philosophies and practices is essential to the long-term perpetuation of Indigenous cultures in the same way that recognition of the power and place of women within tribal Nations is central to Indigenous empowerment.

# Scholarship on the Legacy of Colonialism and Gender Scholarship

## Legacy of Colonialism

Building on prior work on colonialism that recognizes the multidimensional strands of oppression and the interlocking problems and conditions inherent to domination provides a mechanism for examining layered impacts on gendered systems and practices that must be restored, changed, or strengthened, both within Indigenous

---

4. Cangleska, Inc. (2000).

Nations and mainstream society. Recognition of the relationship between worldview and ideology on systems of gender stratification within social organizations is pivotal in examining the shifts that have occurred within Indigenous societies. The recognition of the structural dynamics of oppression that produce and maintain gender inequity at all levels is also recognized by mainstream feminism.[5] Awareness of the relationship between ideology, worldview, and gender is particularly cogent when examining the gendered structural disruption generated by colonialism within Indigenous Nations and the aftermath of these historic events.

## Gender Scholarship

Debates are numerous about feminism and gender-oriented research among women of color. Much of the early gender scholarship documents the pervasive nature of gender stratification in mainstream society, the maintenance and resilience of gender inequity in social structures, and a commitment toward creating equity in gender arrangements.[6] Women of color, often representing the voice of third wave of feminism, have clearly articulated the importance of greater attention to the perspectives and issues of women who are experiencing multiple forms of oppression that compound gender biases with racism, class subordination, heterosexism, and colonialism.[7] The multiple, unidimensional, or interwoven systems of oppression confronting women are inherent to the philosophies and systems that have spawned practices of subjugation. Rejecting analysis in which micro-level interpretations of race, class, and gender oppression are removed from the macro-level contextual experiences of histories of colonization and oppression, Indigenous women and women of color are more likely to argue for integrative gender frameworks and theories that require analysis of the multiple manifestations of oppression in the lives of women. Rather than viewing gender and race as mutually

---

5. Chafetz (1999).
6. Pelak, Taylor, & Whittier (1999)
7. Robbins, Chatterjee, & Canda (1998).

separable categories, Indigenous feminists reject the fragmentation of the issues and instead critique the multilayered dimensions of oppression faced by women of color in negotiating systems of domination. These holistic approaches are consistent with those being advanced by First Nations practitioners and stakeholders addressing VAAIW, as well as Indigenous feminists.

# Dynamics of Oppression and the Response to Mainstream Feminist Theory

The need for integrative frameworks that consider the structural implications of colonization in social work practice in First Nations communities is apparent when considering the dynamics of oppression and the response of First Nations women to mainstream feminist theory. Although practices inherent to colonization and oppression disrupted and often obliterated gendered systems based on reciprocity and egalitarianism, there is an absence in the literature examining the disconnect between these experiences of oppression and concepts of women's rights, gender issues, and feminism as advanced by mainstream feminists. As a result, tribal women who retain cultural practices, gender knowledge, and systems reflective of reciprocity may see little benefit in embracing mainstream feminism that is viewed as being concerned only with the rights of women versus the rights and survival of Nations.

The examination of traditional cultural differences found in the gender dynamics of tribal peoples and the multidimensional shifts resulting from colonization, particularly the imposition of White male-based hierarchies of power and privilege and patriarchal systems are best understood by using integrative frameworks cognizant of structural disruption produced by these experiences of oppression.[8] While mainstream feminist concepts have been use-

---

8. Enloe (2000) discusses the role of militarization in privileging masculine values and the normalization of the subjugation of women.

ful, ongoing debate and discussion about the agenda, responses, and relevance of White feminist theory to First Nations women, specifically, and Third World Indigenous People, generally, has contributed to the emergence of Indigenous feminism and associated feminist analysis.

Rooted in the traditional power, knowledge, and influence of tribal women and gendered systems within First Nations cultures, Indigenous feminism rejects worldviews, systems, and practices predicated on hierarchical power and domination.[9] Initial suspicion of mainstream feminism led some to conclude this movement for gender equity was little more than a diversionary tactic to distract First Nations women from the *real* agenda of decolonization and the accompanying struggles for liberation. Others maintain that feminism is irrelevant to cultures and civilizations based upon egalitarian and matrilineal cultures, with the emphasis on the collective rights of Indigenous Peoples versus the individual rights of women.

Globally, Indigenous women are skeptical about the value of collaborating with women privileged by race, class, access to education, technology, media, funding, and professional opportunities that enable them to control agendas and to assert their point of view over perspectives historically disenfranchised.[10] The different orientations of both mainstream and Indigenous women influence the agenda—the strategies employed as well as the priorities for change. Indigenous women increasingly view violence against women as a human rights violation that cannot be divorced from ongoing colonization and militarism, from racism and social exclusion, and from poverty-inducing economic and "development" policies that have coalesced into a movement of Indigenous women dedicated to the human rights of Indigenous Peoples.[11] Such approaches

---

9. Denetdale (2009) examines the role of militarization in undermining traditional gender practices and the subordination of women under patriarchal systems.

10. Foro Internacional de Mujeres Indigenas (FIMI) [International Indigenous Women's Forum] (2006).

11. Ibid.

are reflected in the document, *Mairin Iwanka Raya: Indigenous Women Stand Against Violence—A Companion Report to the United Nations Secretary-General's Study on Violence Against Women*,[12] which acknowledges:

> *the complex interaction of the combined factors of colonization, the spread of western-style capitalism, globalization, nationalism, and top-down and paternalistic approaches to development [that] have provided a social and economic environment whereby Indigenous women have suffered* (Foro Internacional de Mujeres Indigenas [FIMI] [International Indigenous Women's Forum], 2006, p. 14).

The promotion and imposition of hierarchical systems promoting superiority, privilege, access and voice for some, but not all, are fundamentally flawed in societies with worldviews, philosophies, structures, and systems grounded in egalitarianism, in the collective survival of the People, and in advancement of sovereignty, self-determination, and human rights.

# Critical Need for Analysis of the Structural Effects of Colonization

Without critique of the multiple structural effects of colonization on the gendered roles and systems of Indigenous Nations, as well as the effects of resistance to colonization, Indigenous empowerment will be elusive. It is important to understand the historic and imposed changes that eroded gendered systems within the traditional cultures of First Nations and the effects today. Raising consciousness about the value and strengths of gendered worldviews, systems, practices, and attitudes is a necessary step in the repatriation of power inherent to traditional cultures. Advancing analysis cognizant of the structural elements of colonialism, as well

---

12. Ibid.

as approaches based on strengths and empowerment, is integral to nation-building.

Closer examination of history and its role in disrupting systems using gendered analysis, as well as a strengths-based empowerment framework, becomes one avenue for changing awareness of the effects of colonialism on social systems and conditions faced by tribal peoples today. The treaty-making process into which tribes entered with the colonial and federal government is one example of the many strategies imposed upon Indigenous Peoples to marginalize women. By refusing to recognize female signatories, female heads of households, and clan relationships based on matrilineal principles, the rights of First Nations women in domains such as property, lands, and livestock were abolished as patriarchal systems were imposed upon Indigenous Nations.[13]

# Resilience and Revitalization: Honoring the Power of Resistance

There are tribes, such as the Diné, who were able to resist many of these changes and who retained traditional cultural beliefs and practices, including gendered ceremonies that upheld the power of women. Even in these tribes, however, women have not been fully immune from practices that impose notions of male superiority and privilege and blur traditional cultural beliefs about the role and power of women.[14] Evidence of this disruption can be found in the escalating rates of VAAIW in tribes such as the Diné Nation, long recognized for the strength and beauty of the matrilineal cultures. It is clear that no tribe has been immune from the structural disruption triggered by imperialism and the imposed systems of domination; however, it is equally important to honor the resiliency and resistance that has ensured the persistence of gendered systems and practices within many tribes and led to the revitalization of these practices in others.

---

13. Devens (1992); Shepardson (1995).
14. Denetdale (2009).

Attention to the interwoven threads of the experience of colonization and subjugation and the multiple forces that disrupted Indigenous systems, as well as the critical analysis of these effects and consequences, provides a foundation from which social action and long-term change based on Indigenous empowerment can proceed. Indigenous feminism promotes gendered analysis examining the intersectionality of violence induced by colonialism and oppression and considers the many ways the identities of Indigenous women have been "used as categories for meting out privilege and oppression."[15] Tribal women who have rejected the restrictive and disempowering narratives of oppression throughout history have long borne the brunt of disenfranchisement and marginalization for daring to reject powerlessness. Instead, these women served at the forefront of battles to protect tribal land bases, to defend hunting and fishing rights, to preserve the religious freedom of Indigenous Nations, and to prevent the termination of tribes, among many examples.

# Pivotal Shifts in Mainstream Feminism

The use of integrated analyses advanced in early scholarship by social work activists and feminists of color marked early pivotal shifts in mainstream feminism. Collins described feminism as "a recognition and critique of patriarchy and sexual politics, and their relationship to other class oppressions — capitalism, imperialism, racism and heterosexism — and a set of beliefs, values and ideas about the desired direction for change."[16] These early theoretical frameworks are still relevant in acknowledging the experiences of colonization experienced by Indigenous Peoples and others. These approaches are consistent with Indigenous decolonization and community-based change efforts that recognize the value of traditional

---

15. Foro Internacional de Mujeres Indigenas (FIMI) [International Indigenous Women's Forum] (2006, p. 14).
16. Collins (1986, p. 214).

gender philosophies and systems, including gender reciprocity, and the kinship and clan structures. Understanding the importance of examining the intersections formed through the politics of Western feminism and the politics of Indigenous communities and using frameworks congruent with the agendas found within tribal communities are critical for advancing in advancing Indigenous feminism.

# Reclaiming Indigenous Concepts of Gender for Revitalization

Indigenous women and communities, in the United States and globally, are working toward social change that confronts the relationship between colonization, the adoption of patriarchal systems, and increasing levels of violence against Indigenous women and children. Rather than continuing to adopt and adapt mainstream philosophies, beliefs, and practices, thereby internalizing colonization, indigenous grassroots efforts for social change increasingly challenge the absence of colonialism in discussion of violence against Indigenous women, while promoting the reclamation and restoration of indigenous concepts of gender. Further, this challenge promotes the revitalization of the structures, ceremonies, and socialization practices that support these ideologies as solution to violence against Indigenous women.

# Empowerment Through the Evolution of Indigenous Feminism

Practices that subjugate the knowledge and experiences of historically disempowered populations, who are characterized by marginal status in the social order and the lack of meaningful participation in decision-making processes affecting their future are an inherent feature of systems of domination. These practices do little to advance the sovereignty, self-determination, or agendas of Indigenous People that seek change, but instead serve only to perpetuate structures of oppression. Historically, women, particularly women of color and poor women, have been most vulnerable to political decision-making processes used as a means for controlling or regulating the behavior and bodies of those subjugated by systems of privilege, power, influence, and access to decision-making. For many Indigenous women, the attacks on gendered systems and the philosophies of reciprocity and egalitarianism marked a loss of power and a diminishment of the role and influence of women within increasingly male-dominated hierarchical structures and systems. This systematic diminishment stands in contrasts to the empowerment woven through egalitarian systems in which all genders were equally valued.

Examining the extent to which subordination is shaped by the position of each oppressed group to White men, typically privileged in these structures, becomes paramount to systemic change initiatives. Class, ethnicity, race, gender, ability, and sexual orientation are the markers of group membership used to determine power and become both the basis for rewards and punishments in hierarchical societies. Depending on one's hierarchical proximity to the source of power, the forms of rewards and oppression vary, thus producing different agendas and the potential for conflict, particularly when change is advanced that threatens the status quo.[17] These identities or markers are instrumental in maintaining systems of domination and oppression, as well as the mechanisms for control and rewards. In many ways, these structures serve an important gatekeeping function for the distribution of privilege and status in vertically privileged societies. This entrenchment of hierarchical systems and concepts of entitlement continue to provoke tension and conflict, not only in tribal communities but also throughout societies and nations globally.

Literature on gender-role conflict in the mainstream research examines the consequences of disparity between one's gender roles and the expectations of others based on these roles. Such roles are

17. Hurtado (1997).

defined and transmitted through socialization practices both positively and negatively affecting individual's well-being, with multiple effects on nearly every dimension of a women's life.[18] The intellectual, emotional, physical, and spiritual conflict generated for Indigenous women whose roles, needs, and choices have frequently collided with the ideology of oppression and the systems established within hierarchical structures produce conflict in the interactions of Indigenous women at multiple levels. Gender conflict should not be approached as a *deficit of gender*, but instead as a rejection of structural oppression impeding or restricting the choices and development of women.

The potential for gender conflict among tribal women is premised on the multiple and competing perspectives related to gender role expectations that Indigenous women must confront and negotiate as differing cultural constructions of gender and the aftermath of colonization are mediated and acted upon. Existing mainstream responses and practice with First Nations women on issues such as violence and abuse may be inadequate, culturally irrelevant, or insensitive to the cultural experiences of Indigenous Peoples. Little research with Indigenous women outside of a clinical or deficit perspective has occurred, with even less scholarship on sex roles, the status of women, or gender, particularly from an empowerment perspective.[19]

---

18. Robbins, Chatterjee, & Canda (1998).
19. LaFromboise, Heyle, & Ozer (1990).

# Chapter Four

# Research Paradigms: Best Practices, Mainstream Academic Research, and the Indigenous Approach to Scholarship

*Our program doesn't use the terms* victim *or even* survivors of violence and abuse. *We're* ***not*** *victims or survivors, simply women who've had this experience and are overcoming it* (Anonymous, 2009, personal communication).

## Historical Precedent for Resistance to Mainstream Research

There is a long history and legitimate suspicion of scientific research and medical studies conducted by mainstream researchers on Indigenous Peoples. As discussed by Maori scholar, Linda Tuhiwai Smith, *research* is one of the dirtiest words in the language of Indigenous Peoples, used to justify legitimacy for the imperial invasion and the oppression of First Nations Peoples.[1] Research has been a tool used to extract knowledge and claim ownership of tribal ways of knowing, while First Nations Peoples globally have been

---

1. Smith (1999, p. 1).

denied the right to existence—the rights of self-determination and sovereignty throughout history. The disempowerment of tribal Peoples through research and scientific studies, unethical researchers, and unconscionable research practices has fueled distrust among First Nations.

## Complicity of Social Institutions: Public Health Services, Indian Health Services, and the Bureau of Indian Affairs

The complicity of social institutions in such practices has served to reinforce resistance to research studies affecting the willingness of many tribal people to participate in research projects. The United States Public Health Services, Indian Health Services (IHS), and the Bureau of Indian Affairs (BIA) boarding schools serve as examples of such practices that continued well into the 1970s. The IHS and BIA—federal agencies charged with trust responsibilities for the health and education of tribal peoples—failed to inform kindergarten through twelfth-grade students or their parents about research procedures and studies in which tribal children were subjected to while attending boarding schools. The failure of these federal agencies to exercise minimal oversight in protecting tribal patients, allowed researchers to engage in unethical irresponsible actions, including the utilization of medical practices and procedures that were not considered usual or customary.[2] As a result of the investigation of the sterilization practices of IHS, the United States General Accounting Office investigated IHS abuses of children in BIA-operated boarding schools.[3] The failure of the IHS to protect tribal patients by adherence to well-established protocol for informed consent in medical practices during this same period led to widespread sterilization practices against Indigenous women in IHS clinics, until 1979, when the United States Department of

---

2. Staats (1976).
3. Ibid.

Health, Education and Welfare changed regulations for sterilization practices with tribal women. Representing one of the most egregious examples of medical misconduct against First Nations, conservative estimates suggest up to 42% of American Indian women of childbearing age experienced sterilization without informed or full consent. These genocidal practices are largely unknown to those outside tribal communities[4] but perpetuate reasonable distrust and rejection of scientific and academic research agendas.

## Experimental Data: From the Tuskegee Study to the Havasupai Project

This example of the failure to use informed consent and research misconduct with Indigenous Peoples is not unlike those of other communities of color, including the Tuskegee syphilis experiment conducted by the United States Public Health Service with African American subjects. This research travesty ultimately led to significant changes in research protocol to protect research participants from research abuse.[5] Unfortunately, disreputable research practices did not end in 1979, but continue today. In 2008, the Havasupai Tribe sued Arizona State University (Tempe, AZ) for research misconduct involving studies of the Havasupai between 1990 and 1992 in which more than 200 blood samples were collected from the Havasupai. The researchers claimed to study diabetes, but the samples were improperly transferred to and used by academic researchers and scientists at Arizona State University and other universities to study unrelated topics without informed consent, including schizophrenia, inbreeding, and the prehistoric migration of native peoples from Asia. The Havasupai case is a classic example of those who argue they have not participated in the oppression of Indigenous Peoples, yet continue to benefit from the advantages of ongoing oppression of marginalized populations with impunity. Disreputable research practices that were "good enough" for use

---

4. Carpio (2004).
5. Tuskegee University (2003); Jones (1981).

with the Havasupai produced benefits for university researchers whose professional careers were advanced through tenure and promotion based on this flawed research, as well as graduate students who completed degrees using ill-gotten research generated from the Havasupai project. This lawsuit was recently settled in 2010, with a provision for returning the remaining blood samples to the Havasupai.[6]

The blatant disregard and lack of adherence to professional standards of research when working with historically oppressed populations demonstrate the continued arrogance of mainstream researchers and the ongoing nature of colonization. Research agendas established outside tribal communities — without tribal consent and without input into topics, methods used, or control of data — and the history of research misconduct affect the willingness of tribal governments and communities to participate in research projects, particularly when the benefit of the research to issues faced by tribes is not clearly established.

The significant sociopolitical shifts that occurred in the 1970s produced many early Indigenous scholars and researchers who challenged notions and methods inherent to mainstream research paradigms, and this infusion of research capacity has had some benefits. Tribal governments begin establishing research boards and protocols to protect membership from the unscrupulous practices of academic researchers, as well as using the courts to sue those who engage in unauthorized or unethical research. As tribes begin engaging in research, self-determination, and setting their own priorities and agendas for research, participation has declined in projects driven by the external research agendas of non-tribal university faculty seeking tenure or grant research projects designed by mainstream institutions *for* tribes, without any collaboration or input from those being studied. The lack of long-term commitment to tribes or engagement in research for tribally defined priorities and interests has often been fleeting, with tribal communities left wondering, *Whatever became of that study?*

---

6. Mello & Wolf (2010).

This backdrop, now worsened by the Havasupai project, has intensified tribal mistrust of researchers and led tribal communities to conclude research studies are of little value because the priorities are not set by tribal governments or Indigenous People. It is also clear there are pressing issues facing tribes that require accurate and meaningful data as solutions are identified.

## Tribal Research Paradigms Supporting Collaborative Partnerships in Research

If the stakes were not so high, it would be both understandable for Indigenous Nations and other disenfranchised communities who have experienced such unforgiveable conduct to shut the research door altogether. Instead, tribal governments are increasingly taking control of their research agendas, as well as the regulatory processes for research approval in order to protect intellectual and cultural property rights as well as the citizen of First Nations. Within many Indigenous Nations, researchers are required to receive approval not only from the institutional review board (IRB) of their own academic institution, but also that of the IRB within the tribal Nation in which they intend to conduct research. Other national tribal organizations, such as the National Congress for American Indians (Washington, DC) and the American Indian Higher Education Consortium (Alexandria, VA) are working to build the capacity of research within Indigenous Nations through initiatives increasing the numbers of tribal scholars and researchers committed to advancing an agenda dedicated to the collection and dissemination of tribally relevant research at the national level.

Tribal research paradigms, unlike mainstream research agendas, engage tribal communities in collaborative partnerships with tribes in identifying research priorities and agendas. Stakeholder engagement and ownership in the research processes is a necessary correction of the processes and reduces the risks of research to ensure the Havasupai Project does not occur again. Rather than ending all research, tribes become partners in the development of research capacity and exercise self-determination by setting and controlling their own research agenda. Engaging communities in the processes and partnering with researchers provide an empowering venue for studies that reflect the needs, issues, and concerns of tribal communities versus those determined solely by outside experts. Although considerable progress has been made, emerging tribal researchers in mainstream institutions, particularly at the doctoral level, are still confronted with limited choices when conducting research that comes from an Indigenous perspective. The emphasis on demonstrating proficiency in mainstream knowledge systems and research rather than protocol steeped in the diversity of Indigenous knowledge systems, values, and beliefs produces an academic and cultural dilemma for Indigenous students committed to Indigenous ways of knowing that is too frequently irreconcilable.[7]

## Indigenous Scholarship Redefining Research Methodology

Several pivotal research reports by Indigenous scholars and allies have contributed to an emerging Indigenous knowledge base and culturally relevant research methodology in the field of violence and abuse against Indigenous women (VAAIW). Equally important elements of the research design, methodology, and process of existing approaches have been advanced in this scholarship. When examined broadly, this body of work represents a synthesis of promising new approaches for culturally viable future research on the topic of violence against Indigenous women. By selecting research methods congruent with principles of engagement, collaboration, and Indigenous strengths and multidimensionality within the community of First Nations helpers, practitioners, organizers, and activists, these projects establish significant founda-

---

7. Peacock, George, Wilson, et al. (2003).

tions upon which future research with First Nations can be approached. Methods that exemplify value and respect for Indigenous sovereignty and self-determination as demonstrated by the processes and methods used are critical in the work of the capacity-building underway in tribal Nations.

*Institutional Ethnography Methods.* Using methodologies that incorporate Indigenous systems of knowledge and methodology, researchers in the first project used *institutional ethnography methods* in a culturally rich study of the impact of processes inherent to the justice systems on tribal women who had experienced violence and abuse.[8] Five basic principles inherent to Indigenous systems of knowledge guided the research and interpretation of the results. These principles are:

1) *Communality of knowledge;*
2) *Value of recognizing and honoring spiritual connections;*
3) *Relational accountability;*
4) *Reciprocity;* and
5) *Holism.*

This study concluded "that a system must honor all our relationships, be holistic and respect women in order to have integrity for Indigenous People and communities."[9] Numerous recommendations were identified to address the "dangerous disjuncture" in the way institutional practices and processes within the legal and judicial systems unfold that effectively derail the attention from the *simultaneous and interrelated needs* of tribal Nations to those of the institution.

*Community Readiness Model.* A second research project examined the willingness of Indigenous communities to address violence and abuse using the *community readiness model.*[10] Fifteen tribal communities who received funding from the Violence Against

---

8. Ibid.
9. Ibid, p. 247.
10. Thurman, Bubar, Plested, et al. (2003).

Women Act[11] and/or grants from the STOP (Services-Training-Officers-Prosecutors) Violence Against Women Grant Program[12] were initially included in this study conducted by the Tri-Ethnic Center for Prevention Research (Fort Collins, CO). Several findings were identified to effectively address violence, including approaches that:

1) Meaningfully engage multiple systems to produce effective and sustainable community mobilization;
2) Build on the utilization of strengths, resources, and capacity within communities;
3) Address the historical issues;
4) Are culturally relevant; and
5) Are oriented toward long-term change or capacity-building.

*STOP (Services-Training-Officers-Prosecutors) Grant Programs: Best Practices.* The final research report funded by the United States Department of Justice, evaluated activities of tribally based STOP Grant Programs and identified *best practices* developed by these programs.[13] Strengths and obstacles in the grant activities provided by these programs were assessed in these areas:

- Program activities and innovations;
- Codes and ordinances;
- Law enforcement;
- Court system and prosecution;
- Survivor services;
- Program coordination and data collection; and
- Agency training and community education.

---

11. Violence Against Women Act (VAWA) (1994); VAWA—Victims of Trafficking and Violence Protection Act (2000); Violence Against Women and Department of Justice Reauthorization Act (2005).

12. Thurman, Bubar, Plested, et al. (2003); United States Department of Justice, Office of Violence Against Women (n.d.).

13. United States Department of Justice, Office of Violence Against Women (n.d.).

Evaluators of these STOP Grant Programs identified best practices for projects, which included:

- Activities that promote changes in values and beliefs about violence against Indian women; and
- Changing or strengthening structures and procedures for responding to violence, including:
  - Crossing tribal and non-tribal boundaries and jurisdictions to create coordinated community responses; and
  - Development of culturally appropriate services and programs that build on tribal resources and community needs, including re-education programs for batterers and coordination with alcohol and drug programs.

# Research on Violence and Abuse against Women (VAAW)

This section describes the research processes typically used in mainstream research that served to support the author's original 2004 dissertation study on violence and abuse against college-age Indigenous women.[14] This discussion is intended to familiarize those who may be unfamiliar with quantitative research of the processes used in conducting research and to provide a critical examination of the lessons learned as well as a general discussion of the research process for students entering research tract disciplines, particularly Indigenous students and others who may have interest in alternative methods of research, but little, if any exposure to methods of research being advanced by First Nations scholars. Conclusions about the benefits to tribal governments and organizations interested in establishing data baselines for use in tracking VAAIW and the success of interventions in ending this phenomenon can be drawn by the reader.

---

14. Chenault (2004).

## Best Practices Research: Mainstream Academic Research and the Indigenous Approach to Scholarship

One of the early steps taken among academic researchers is to identify a research question of interest and to engage in an exhaustive review of the existing scholarship in order to determine best practices for prevailing social problems, as well as the gaps in the research for which new studies are proposed. These findings provide insight into what is known, as well as what has been learned from prior studies about best practices within a given field. The term *best practices research* describes studies that objectively evaluate evidence of success in interventions and provide direction for those seeking to improve or develop quality programs and services. Rather than "reinventing the wheel," this research theoretically enables practitioners to improve or advance approaches and practice in a given field while providing activists with the data and literature needed for policy advocacy to address social problems, such as violence against women.

While these approaches are standard elements of mainstream academic research, Indigenous researchers maintain investigations that start in the abstract terrain of professional discourse and literature reviews can be viewed as inconsistent with Indigenous research methods increasingly advanced by tribal scholars. Approaches that reinforce disconnection and fragmentation at multiple levels are increasingly replaced in tribal communities by emerging methods that situate power in the lives, words, and experiences of Indigenous Peoples, as well as the vantage point of those whose experience is essential in guiding and informing the relevance of research to change, such as VAAIW.[15]

***Conflict for Indigenous Graduate Students and Faculty.*** Research is thus not isolated from the forces of oppression and practices of mainstream social institutions, but instead a means for privileging select research methods and the subjugation of others. It is not un-

---

15. Peacock, George, Wilson, et al. (2003).

common for Indigenous graduate students preparing to conduct research to grapple with agonizing decisions about the use of accepted Western knowledge systems and methods, or to engage in renegade research, using methods valuing Indigenous perspectives, practices, and policies. These ethical and culturally based dilemmas can take an extraordinary toll on the aspirations of First Nations graduate students and non-tenured tribal faculty—forced to engage in battle with the academy when arguing for the relevance and validity of innovative culturally based approaches. Disillusionment with the level of entrenchment in these systems has halted the completion of doctoral research for innumerable Indigenous scholars in the final stage of research for doctoral programs and likely had an impact on tenure and promotion decisions for countless other First Nations scholars. While the "path of least resistance" frequently advocated is to "jump through the [required] hoops" until one has fulfilled the requirements and completed the degree, for others the challenge is to acquire expertise in the requisite knowledge and skills necessary to understand and navigate Western systems while retaining one's indigenousness and commitment to the sovereignty of tribal peoples extracts a heavy toll. The luxury of engaging in, or publishing academic research fully situated in an Indigenous perspective or ways of knowing, is not a common experience but instead exclusive, often limited to those who have earned tenure and privilege in these hierarchical systems by producing work fulfilling mainstream standards of excellence.

## Literature Review: 1977 to 2004 in Psychology, Sociology, and Social Work Databases

A review of the literature was conducted from 1977 to 2004 using psychology, sociology, and social work databases to identify research on the topic of violence against Indigenous women was an initial step in the research process. For inclusion in this review, the key criteria for articles were based on the use of research methods that tested the benefit of interventions used with women who had experienced violence and abuse. This approach was influenced by a desire to know what has been proven to work with women, particularly Indigenous women who had experienced violence and abuse. Rather than using a qualitative research design that interviewed tribal women who had experienced violence and abuse, the decision was made to use a quantitative research design based on the research questions posed about the prevalence and incidence of VAAIW and the effects of violence and abuse on women's power. Because these questions were best investigated by using larger samples and statistical tests to examine differences in women who had experienced violence compared with those who had not, a quantitative method seemed appropriate at the time of the study. Prior anecdotal research conducted on the topic in the 1970s had been largely dismissed by academics, and the decision to use quantitative methods was an effort to ensure the results were not ignored on this basis, as well as charting a path for quantitative researchers with an interest in the topic and conceptual framework advanced.

The literature review focused on empirical studies examining interventions used with women who have experienced violence. Theoretically, this approach sounds plausible; however, such interventions are difficult to implement when services are being provided in time-limited shelter settings and to women in crises. The short-term nature of stays in violence shelters, the more important issues of survival and change that consume the attention of women in such situations, as well as shelter-staff turnover, creates tremendous challenges for programs to engage in such research. Often confronted with a rapidly changing group of women in shelter settings, limited research capacity, and funding requirements that mandate comprehensive data collection to maintain funding eligibility, these programs are frequently in between the proverbial rock and a hard place in demonstrating change or improvement using the funding acquired.

Determining best practices from the research literature as mainstream professionals are trained to do is equally problematic. Although thousands of articles on violence against women exist in the social science literature, the number of abstracts drastically thinned when keywords related to outcomes associated with evaluation of the effectiveness of an intervention were added. When search terms such as *best practices, empirical research, evaluation,* or *interventions,*

with the terms *American Indian, Native American, Indians of American, Indigenous People, First Nations* were used with the terms *domestic violence, battering, violence and abuse against women,* the number of articles dramatically declined. While there are thousands of articles addressing VAAW and many more describing or conceptualizing the impacts of such experiences on women, there is little actual research documenting interventions that are most successful for women, including tribal women who have experienced violence and abuse. In fact, it was so unbelievable that a manual review of 3,000 abstracts that fit the original parameters of the study and a review of government documents accessible online was conducted to ensure nothing had been missed in the initial electronic searches for an earlier study in 2004.

## Results of Literature Review

It was astounding to learn that after decades of work on violence and women, there were only eight articles[16] that fit the criteria from 1986 to 2000, with only two of these eight including any Indigenous women in the sample.[17] This chapter describes the broad patterns of the research in this field, using an empowerment framework in an effort to highlight what is known about what works, as well as the consistency of these efforts with empowerment practice. These findings were then woven into the construction of a quantitative study on VAAIW, which also integrated the practice wisdom and approaches of First Nations programs using empowerment frameworks.

The bulk of empirical research on violence and abuse has been limited to domestic violence or intimate partner violence and is

---

16. Berk, Newton, & Berk (1986); Cox & Stoltenberg (1991); Mancoske, Standifer & Cauley (1994); Rubin (1991); Shamai (2000); Tutty (1993; 1996); Tutty, Bidgood & Rothery (1993).

17. The two studies that included First Nations women were Mancoske, Standifer & Cauley (1994) and Tutty (1996). The Mancoske study included two Indigenous women; the Tutty study included eight First Nations women.

primarily conducted in shelter settings or through follow-up services after women leave shelters. This research examines the effects of practice interventions on selected outcomes associated with abusive intimate relationships to determine which interventions or treatment benefited women, based on statistically significant findings. *Statistical significance* is a research term describing findings attributed to an intervention or treatment being tested, rather than change based on random chance, with the goal being to link interventions to statistically significant findings. *Cultural significance* is a term advanced in this work to denote important cultural findings to Indigenous Peoples that may or may not be statistically significant to academic researchers.

The interventions tested in these eight studies[18] included numerous practice approaches commonly used in the field of violence and abuse including: *cognitive therapy, grief counseling, feminist counseling, outreach counseling, structured* and *unstructured support groups,* and *follow-up groups.* It is important to point out the findings described are based on a limited set of studies conducted with relatively small numbers of women. Of these eight studies, seven were quantitative studies,[19] with one qualitative study.[20] The largest study of the seven quantitative studies included 243 women.[21] A total of 312 women participated in the remaining six studies,[22] with an average of 52 participants in each study. From a research standpoint, these limitations affect the ability to generalize or apply the findings of these studies to all women who have experienced violence and abuse. Practice approaches that demonstrate both sta-

---

18. Berk, Newton, & Berk (1986); Cox & Stoltenberg (1991); Mancoske, Standifer & Cauley (1994); Rubin (1991); Shamai (2000); Tutty (1993; 1996); Tutty, Bidgood & Rothery (1993).

19. Berk, Newton, & Berk (1986); Cox & Stoltenberg (1991); Mancoske, Standifer & Cauley (1994); Rubin (1991); Tutty (1993; 1996); Tutty, Bidgood & Rothery (1993).

20. Shamai (2000).

21. Berk, Newton, & Berk (1986).

22. Cox & Stoltenberg (1991); Mancoske, Standifer, & Cauley (1994); Rubin (1991); Tutty (1993; 1996); Tutty, Bidgood & Rothery (1993).

tistically significant and consistent findings exemplify best practices and contribute to the knowledge base within a particular field of study, such as violence against women. Although the number of studies was limited, the statistically significant findings in these studies suggest that the interventions produced positive changes in the self-esteem, self-efficacy, and social support of women and merit additional attention; however, again, it would be an error to attempt to generalize the findings to all women who have experienced violence and abuse because of the limited numbers of studies and overall sample size. While two additional studies identified women of color in the sample,[23] the success of these outcomes specifically with women of color is equally unclear, however promising these outcomes appear in existing studies. As noted, a variety of interventions were being tested to determine the effectiveness of these approaches in working with women who had experienced violence and abuse.

Two Canadian studies contained small numbers of Indigenous women participants in the samples.[24] In the 1996 Tutty study, 60 Canadian women, which included eight First Nations women, participated in a mixed method design to evaluate the efficacy of follow-up programs for abused women.[25] The women who participated in this study completed standardized measures on social support, self-esteem, and perceived stress as they entered the follow-up program and again 3 months later. These findings reported statistically significant improvement in self-esteem as well as appraisal or social support when ongoing follow-up programs are available to women who have experienced violence and abuse. This study suggests the self-esteem and perceptions of social support are enhanced by interventions that recognize recovery from violence requires multiple changes and adjustments, with different needs at various stages of life, which may or may not be met through time-limited shelter programs. It affirms the importance of providing women in tran-

---

23. Berk, Newton & Berk (1986); Cox & Stoltenberg (1991).
24. Mancoske, Standifer, & Cauley (1994); Tutty (1996).
25. Tutty (1996).

sition with meaningful opportunities to talk about their experiences, to have their voices heard, and to reconnect to systems of support to facilitate recovery from the multiple traumas of violence and abuse as a strategy for empowerment.[26] Approaches that counter the effects of violence and abuse on self-esteem and social support are commonly viewed as integral to the process of recovery or healing from such experiences.

The second Canadian study including Indigenous women evaluated the effectiveness of a brief counseling approach, paired with two types of social work counseling services.[27] With a sample of 20 women, including two First Nations women, this study used a comparative treatment design, in which the participants were randomly assigned to one of two interventions: either a grief resolution counseling approach or a feminist counseling approach. Standardized measures of self-esteem, self-efficacy, and attitudes towards feminism were used to evaluate the efficacy of practice. Overall improvements for all participants were reported; however, analysis of the data by counseling type reported statistically significant improvements in self-esteem and self-efficacy using the grief resolution counseling approach. The effect of violence and abuse in lowering the self-esteem of women has long been examined and is supported by empirical research.[28] Negative perceptions related to self-esteem and self-efficacy are considered to be *consequences of victimization* rather than inherent character flaws that dispose women to experiences of violent victimization.[29] Self-efficacy or the belief that one has the ability to produce and regulate events in life lends itself to initiative and confidence in taking empowering action.[30] Practice that supports women as they grieve multiple losses that result from violence victimization, including loss of self-esteem and self-efficacy, are additional and important practice issues that must be addressed as one recovers self.

---

26. Busch & Valentine (2000); Shamai, (2000).
27. Mancoske, Standifer, & Cauley (1994).
28. Carlson (1977); Fleming (1979); Hartick (1982); Tutty (1993).
29. Tutty (1993).
30. Bandura (1983); Robbins, Chatterjee, & Canda (1998).

*Construct of Self-Esteem.* Within the mainstream literature and research on *self-esteem*, the concept is used to describe *the positive or negative regard one has about oneself or one's overall worth or value.* Strong or positive self-esteem is associated with many positive attributes, including one's confidence, strength, and resilience in overcoming adversity. From an empowerment perspective, *self-esteem — the attitudes, beliefs, and perceptions one has about self —* is associated with personal empowerment. An empowerment approach to self-esteem would suggest that, in order to own one's power, or to take power back, the attitudes and beliefs that influence one's self-perception must be challenged, strengthened, or reinforced as needed. Individuals who think and believe they have no value, no worth, and no options are effectively disempowered by these attitudes and beliefs, as well as by conditions and circumstances that give rise to such hopelessness.

The negative effects of violence and abuse on self-esteem are commonly identified in the literature on violence against women and focused on in intervention and shelter programs. This common outcome was tested across the studies in the intervention research.[31] One tool of oppression associated with VAAW is that of emotional abuse. The self-esteem of women who are yelled at and made to feel that they are worthless, stupid, or inadequate, or that they have caused the violence experienced, are adversely affected by the emotional abuse experienced. From an empowerment perspective, emotional violence and abuse that negatively affect one's attitudes, beliefs, and perceptions about self are disempowering. A person consistently subjected to emotional abuse is effectively being brainwashed into believing they have no value or worth in order to justify treatment and conditions that reinforce a sense of powerlessness.

Although it makes sense that violence and abuse affect self-esteem, the small number of overall studies that have actually tested this hypothesis limit the ability of research-based practitioners to generalize such findings to all women who have experienced vio-

---

31. Berk, Newton and Berk (1986).

lence and abuse. This limitation does not mean there have not been studies exploring the relationship between violence and abuse and self-esteem or that the findings of these studies are not important. From a research standpoint, there are simply not enough research studies to conclude the findings apply to all women. Researchers do not conclusively know:

- Whether the self-esteem of all women is affected by violence and abuse in the same way;
- Whether violence and abuse has short-term or lasting effects on self-esteem;
- Whether mainstream definitions for self-esteem and the measures of self-esteem typically used in the existing studies accurately reflect the way Indigenous women define self-esteem; or
- Whether self-esteem is an element of the power of Indigenous women.

These gaps in the research provide a case for further examination to ensure the focus of work with women who have experienced violence is accurately targeting the critical domains, without disenfranchising women whose power may be shaken but not destroyed.

There is a need to design research surveys and measures that can accurately measure more complex constructs as well as accurately define and measure constructs from an Indigenous perspective and the use of rigorous and culturally sound approaches. In the absence of such shifts, the research norm is a reliance on existing mainstream measures designed for populations that may not be valid for work with Indigenous Peoples and other communities of culture. Researchers are effectively measuring concepts that may be defined differently in tribal communities or have little relevance within these populations.

One could rightfully argue that approaches which assume the self-esteem of women is damaged and that self-esteem needs to be "fixed" before any meaningful recovery from violence can occur is a *deficit approach*. Failing to acknowledge the strength and resiliency of women in overcoming adversity or the structural forces supporting the oppression of women is too often absent in research studies, for many reasons. The comments of one young tribal woman epitomizes common sentiments of Indigenous women who reject *victim-blaming approaches*:

> Our program doesn't use the terms *victim* or even *survivors of violence and abuse*. We're **not** victims or survivors, simply women who've had this experience and have overcome it.—Anonymous (2009, personal communication).

Research designs and methods that fail to consider the knowledge, voice, and experience of Indigenous women; the multidimensional factors influencing the conditions of Indigenous Peoples today; and the strengths and resiliency of tribal peoples, as well as the importance of engaging communities in research, can be especially problematic for those committed to empowerment and social justice.

*Construct of Social Support and Interpersonal Empowerment.* Another of the constructs explored in the 2004 study is *social support*.[32] Both self-esteem and social support were selected for use in this study in an effort to understand the effect of violence and abuse on the power of women and whether existing constructs for empowerment would be useful in understanding the power of Indigenous women. For all of the reasons previously discussed, the usefulness of the measures and definitions of these terms may or may have limited value with tribal women; however, these measures are the most commonly used of the constructs available.

*Social support* describes *the level of support one has available for overcoming crises and dealing with life problems or circumstances of adversity, as well as the level of support one is able to offer others.* Again, social support is a common outcome in this set of violence studies and an outcome targeted for change by programs responding to violence against women. *Social support* and a *sense of belonging* are considered protective factors that enable individuals to respond to or overcome stressful or traumatic circumstances. Without adequate social support, it is believed individuals may be more vulnerable in crises or less successful in overcoming crises. From an

---

32. Chenault (2004).

empowerment perspective, the quality and quantity of connections one has with others and the ability to influence circumstances by accessing help or resources, or in helping others to do the same, is described as *interpersonal empowerment*. Individuals who have the knowledge and skills necessary to navigate service systems, to advocate and access resources for themselves and others, and to utilize a range of support available, are engaged in the use of their power, not only for self, but to help others.

It is not unusual for women to be isolated from family and friends to maintain the dynamics of control and domination present in violence and abuse. Without interference or accountability for violence, the power of the person responsible for the violence is reinforced and the power and control of women is subjugated. This process severs connections to family, friends, and other potential allies while separating both partners from valuable social support networks, resources for support, and accountability within community. Tribal women who are geographically isolated from support may be particularly vulnerable to multiple layers of social isolation because of the remoteness of location, long distances to resources, a lack of access to services, including no transportation, no telephone or wireless communication, and no programs providing services. In tribal communities in which extended networks of support inform one's sense of belonging and place in the community, the tactic of isolation not only reduces the social support available to women, it also undermines the cultural role and responsibilities of both women and men in the community. The inability to participate in community and gendered systems that are vital to the cultural foundation of Indigenous communities has impacts on the vitality of these cultural institutions, as well as the individual who is exiled from this participation. The value derived from engagement in culture and community is consistent with the constructs of social support and sense of belonging, although not established in the literature or existing research measures. Acts of domination and oppression that weaken or destroy the confidence, resiliency, strength, belonging, and support for women are disempowering at multiple levels and likely have ripple effects throughout systems within tribal communities.

*Brief Counseling Approach: Grief Resolution Counseling or Feminist Counseling.* The second study that included Indigenous women evaluated the effectiveness of a *brief counseling approach*, paired with two types of social work counseling services.[33] With a sample of 20 women, including two First Nations women, this study used a comparative treatment design, in which participants were randomly assigned to one of two interventions, a *grief resolution counseling approach* or a *feminist counseling approach*. Standardized measures of self-esteem, self-efficacy, and attitudes toward feminism were used to evaluate which approach produced the best results. Overall improvements for all participants were reported; however, data analysis by the type of counseling received showed statistically significant improvements in self-esteem and self-efficacy using the grief resolution counseling approach.

*Construct of Self-Efficacy.* The effect of violence and abuse in lowering the self-esteem of women has been examined and is supported by empirical research. Negative perceptions related to self-esteem and self-efficacy are considered to be *consequences of victimization*. *Self-efficacy* or *the belief that one has the ability to produce and regulate life events* lends itself to initiative and confidence in taking empowering action.[34] These findings suggest practices that support women as they grieve multiple losses from experiences of violence and abuse, including self-esteem and self-efficacy, are important issues that need to be considered to facilitate recovery from violence and abuse. The relationship between self-esteem and self-efficacy with engagement in community or political action is not addressed by existing research, although such approaches are common in Indigenous programs and responses to violence and abuse against Indian women. This approach addresses each of the dimensions associated with empowerment as discussed and described in the literature.

*Reported Improvements in Self-Esteem, Self-Efficacy, and Sense of Belonging or Social Support.* Four[35] of the seven quantitative

---

33. Mancoske, Standifer, & Cauley (1994).
34. Bandura (1982).
35. Cox (1991); Mancoske, Standifer, & Cauley (1994); Tutty (1996); Tutty, Bidgood & Rothery (1993).

studies[36] reported improvements in self-esteem, self-efficacy, and sense of belonging or social support, with three of these four studies reporting statistically significant improvements in self-esteem, self-efficacy, or social support.[37] In addition, a qualitative study[38] identified the importance of creating supportive environments in which women feel they belong and experience a sense of legitimacy in their feelings, thoughts, and desires. This support and sense of belonging enabled women to engage in a process of healing and discovering self or empowerment. These findings and the measures used were then considered in the design of a 2004 study[39] examining the effects of violence and abuse against Indigenous college students on constructs associated with empowerment.

*Prevalence and Frequency Research.* An emerging body of studies examining the prevalence and incidence of VAAIW in health-care settings was also identified.[40] These studies are not only important for establishing the scope of the problem experienced by First Nations women but also provide further evidence of the growing disconnect from the traditional cultural teachings and philosophies. These studies were conducted in tribally operated health-care settings and report rates of emotional abuse ranging from 14% to 18% for past-year incidents of emotional abuse, with physical abuse rates of 42% for tribal women seeking routine health care at a tribal health facility.[41] Lifetime incidents of verbal and physical abuse in a second study in a tribal health-clinic setting were reported by 75% of the participants.[42] Documentation of the rates and fre-

---

36. Berk, Newton, & Berk (1986); Cox & Stoltenberg (1991); Mancoske, Standifer & Cauley (1994); Rubin (1991); Tutty (1993; 1996); Tutty, Bidgood & Rothery (1993).

37. Mancoske, Standifer, & Cauley (1994); Tutty (1996); Tutty, Bidgood & Rothery (1993).

38. Shamai (2000).

39. Chenault (2004).

40. Bohn (2002); Fairchild, Fairchild, & Stoner (1998); Harwell, Moore, & Spence (2003); Malcoe, Duran & Montgomery (2004); Robin, Chester & Rasmussen (1998).

41. Fairchild, Fairchild, & Stoner (1998).

42. Fairchild, Fairchild, & Stoner (1998); Robin, Chester, & Rasmussen (1998).

quency of violence and abuse in health-care systems serving tribal peoples should also be considered from a layered standpoint, which includes cultural philosophies, gender knowledge, practices, and systems that are specifically related to pregnancy and Indigenous women.

In a study of pregnant First Nations women, 90% reported they had experienced emotional, physical, or sexual abuse in their lifetimes, with 33% reporting physical or sexual abuse during the current pregnancy.[43] In two studies of pregnant and childbearing Indigenous women, more than 50% of the sample (58%) in one study[44] reported experiencing physical or sexual intimate-partner violence, and the second study[45] reported the lowest rates of physical violence, with 5% of the sample experiencing such violence and abuse. These findings further evidence structural and cultural disruption and the destabilization of socialization processes in which gendered teachings are transmitted about women and the treatment of pregnant women as understood by tribal peoples. This breakdown in passing knowledge compromises the health and safety of pregnant women and the unborn, family systems, community cohesion, and the cultures of tribal peoples. These gaps in knowledge of those engaging in such violence against pregnant woman can be addressed by families and other social institutions within in tribal communities, including programs responding to VAAIW in order to reverse this cycle for Indigenous Nations committed to cultural sovereignty.

*Value of Statistical Data.* The use of statistics, alone, in reporting rates of VAAIW is not always highly valued, particularly among grassroots activists and practitioners who rightfully maintain that action should move beyond just statistics. While there is merit to this position, there are benefits of data. The use of statistics, such as those discussed, provides tribal governments, organizations, communities, practitioners, and activists with important baseline data to establish the scope of the problem, to use in budgetary and

---

43. Bohn (2002).
44. Malcoe, Duran, & Montgomery (2004).
45. Harwell, Moore, & Spence (2003).

strategic planning decisions for addressing these issue, and to fulfill grant reporting that generates additional revenue for addressing issues such as violence against Indigenous women. Equally important, these numbers provide compelling evidence of the extent to which the traditional cultural teachings have been disrupted so that conscious capacity-building and strategies for social action and change can occur to address the cultural dynamics of Indigenous nation-building.

## Cultural Teachings and Gendered Practices: Shared Diversity among Tribes

Although tremendous disruption of gendered systems and gendered knowledge has occurred, it must also be acknowledged that many tribes have successfully retained and use the cultural teachings and gendered practices. These systems, as well as the knowledge and practices supporting these structures may be useful for tribes whose cultural teachings have been devastated but are being repatriated, despite the great diversity that exists across tribes. Embedded within these systems and knowledge are teachings about the practices required to ensure the well-being of the mother and child that are as valuable today as they were in the past. To correct an imbalance, tribes may conduct ceremonies differently; however, *the intent is often the same.* This starting point may enable tribes to repatriate and revitalize traditions and practices that were left behind on the road of colonization to utilize in correcting the dysfunction represented by VAAIW.

For many tribal peoples, physical or sexual violence against a pregnant women defiles the sacredness of women and the cultural teachings associated with pregnancy, yet too often this knowledge is not being taught, is not used, or is no longer valued. To correct these conditions — the gaps and disruption caused by the colonization experience of Indigenous Peoples — the truth must be honestly spoken. The studies reporting high rates of violence and abuse during pregnancy are useful in the healing processes within tribal communities because these numbers identify the scope of a previously unrecognized high-risk period for tribal women and raises awareness of the urgent need to counter this phenomenon with social action. While there are many strengths and resources within the cultural traditions of Indigenous Peoples and promising practices promoting the revitalization of socialization practices for the genders, these efforts will not be fully successful without the participation and engagement of tribal communities in the multiple layers of work to end violence and abuse in families and communities.

*Indigenous Practice: Healing-Focused Culturally Based Empowerment.* Since the 1970s, Indigenous programs have initiated culturally based strategies for ending VAAIW. These approaches integrate cultural/spiritual philosophies, traditional healing practices, and the use of gendered teachings in work with tribal women, communities, and those who engage in violence. Practice in tribal settings frequently incorporates the analysis of colonization and the structural disruption created by colonialism. This practice is unique because the strengths of tribal cultures and the structural dynamics of Indigenous colonization ground the work with women and tribal communities. These approaches move away from a pathology orientation to what is best described as *culturally based empowerment practice focused on healing communities and capacity-building or nation-building.* Studies evaluating the effectiveness of these approaches have not been reported in the mainstream literature at this time, although each of the three dimensions of empowerment previously identified are anecdotally reported and evidenced (i.e., the personal, interpersonal, and community/political spheres). If one were unfamiliar with the grassroots movements for change within many tribal communities and relied solely upon mainstream journal articles to inform practice, one might mistakenly assume that Indigenous Nations were not responding to VAAIW.

Instead, integrated tribally based interventions strengthen the self-perceptions, knowledge, and skills of community members using social and community action as a mechanism for building on the strengths, capacities, and resources of Indigenous women and their communities. These approaches become a means for reconnecting women with their power, serving as exemplars of culturally based empowerment practice. Natural support networks that were once banned, including gendered practices and systems, are being revived to reconnect and support women as well as men. Responses to violence being used today in tribal communities acknowledge structural disruption and emphasize the key role of women in the cultures upon which Indigenous civilizations were based. For example, in northern New Mexico, women of the Tewa Pueblos have turned to their cultural roots to address rape and sexual violence through a project known as *VOICES* or *Valuing Our Integrity with Courage, Empowerment and Support,* which brings women together around social and cultural activities.[46]

*Valuing Our Integrity with Courage, Empowerment and Support (VOICES).* A shared feature of these programs focuses on healing the "sacred hoop" (the individual, family, and Indigenous nations) by stressing that family violence is not a tradition with First Nations cultures.[47] In these programs, Indigenous women come together in non-threatening women's circles to informally connect with communities of tribal women for support and to acquire cultural knowledge and skills and to use the skills acquired to benefit other women and children facing violence and abuse. Consciousness of the strengths of cultural teachings related to women, relationships, family, and communities are promoted in informal gatherings, while also bonding women with culturally based natural support systems. This use of culture by tribal programs and practitioners responds to issues such as violence and abuse, while also ensuring the perpetuation of cultures that must be lived in order to survive.

*White Buffalo Calf Woman Society.* Tribally appropriate healing practices and resources for the treatment of women who have experienced violence, those who engage in violence against women, and communities are used to facilitate social change and reinforce social systems within tribes at multiple levels. Programs such as

---

46. Tewa Women United (Santa Fe, NM) (2010); available at: http://www.tewawomenunited.org.

47. Ibid.

the White Buffalo Calf Woman Society, Inc. (Mission, SD) of the Lakota Nation provide opportunities for women and men as well as communities to engage in healing practices and develop a range of skills and knowledge as well as provide meaningful opportunities to participate in activities to effect positive social change in families and communities.[48] By relying on cultural practices, including the use of sweat lodges, talking circles, ceremonies, and traditional cultural teachings, awareness of the extent to which worldviews, philosophies, and practices of oppression that feed societal and cultural misogynism are countered. Women and men reclaim power by participating in political and/or community action, reaffirming women's power and role in tribal societies, and utilizing cultural practices for resolving difference.

*Kizhaay Anishinaabe Niin—I Am a Kind Man.* Increasingly, First Nations throughout the United States and Canada are utilizing culturally strengths and resources to build capacity for strong Nations by re-socializing Indigenous men who have adopted misogynistic attitudes and behaviors. Using the Seven Grandfather Teachings of the Ojibway that provide instructions on living in harmony with Creation, this approach to addressing violence and abuse incorporates cultural values and teachings about wisdom, love, respect, bravery, honesty, humility, and truth into its approach. Using traditional cultural practices, the goals of Kizhaay Anishinaabe Niin[49] are to:

- Provide education for men to address issues of abuse against women;
- Re-establish traditional responsibilities by acknowledging that our teachings have never tolerated violence and abuse towards women;
- Inspire men to engage other men to get involved and stop the abuse; [and]
- Support Aboriginal men who choose not to use violence.

---

48. White Buffalo Calf Woman Society (Mission, SD) (n.d.); available at: http://www.wbcws.org.

49. Kizhaay Anishinaabe Niin / I am a Kind Man (Ontario, Canada) (n.d.); available at: http://www.iamakindman.ca/IAKM.

*Summary of Shared Teachings and Practices.* The best practices for healing exemplified by each of these Indigenous approaches are equally significant in addressing the grief and trauma that are often magnified for First Nations women and men and other oppressed populations. The structural disruption produced by colonization in Indigenous communities has contributed to unresolved historical trauma and grief,[50] post-traumatic stress,[51] and depression and violence.[52] First Nations women experience multiple layers of grief as they simultaneously negotiate processes of decolonization and violence and abuse. Acknowledging and grieving experiences associated with the trauma of colonization, oppression, and injustice reduces the self-blame, shame, and the sense of craziness that oppressed people can experience when oppression is denied or trivialized. Such practice is supportive of decolonizing interventions that reconnect marginalized Peoples to the strengths, capacity, and resources needed for nation-building within disenfranchised communities, including Indigenous communities.[53] Practice aligned with multiple layers of grieving and the transitions required to renew strengths, to revitalize resources, and to build upon the capacities of individuals, families, communities, and society is supported by the research and often addressed in tribally based programs.

Interventions that engage clients and community stakeholders in the process of identifying the constellation of issues produced by the historical and contemporary forces of subjugation are essential as social change is promoted. This cornerstone of tribal responses to violence against women guides a wide range of approaches targeting the individual, family, and community. Cangleska, Inc.,[54] and the White Buffalo Calf Woman Society[55] have successfully used

---

50. Brave Heart (1998); Brave Heart & DeBruyn (1998); Weaver & Brave Heart (1999).

51. Duran & Duran (1995); Napoleon (1991); Yellow Bird (2000).

52. LaFromboise, Berman, & Sohi (1994); LaFromboise, Heyle, & Ozer (1990).

53. GlenMaye (1998); Hodges, Burwell, & Ortega (1998).

54. Cangleska, Inc. (2000).

55. White Buffalo Calf Woman Society (Mission, SD) (n.d.); available at: http://www.wbcws.org.

community education and political action strategies to mobilize communities to elect tribal candidates who support zero violence platforms and in efforts to promote tribal codes on violence against Indigenous women. While tribal women who have experienced violence and abuse must be supported and are supported, these programs recognize the structural roots of the problem that must be simultaneously addressed. Raising consciousness and engaging in action to bring about change in the structural dynamics supporting violence and abuse, as well as challenging conditions of classism, racism, patriarchy, heterosexism, sexism, colonialism, and imperialism are equally important. These approaches are equally valuable to other oppressed and marginalized individuals, classes, communities and populations that have historically borne the brunt of such conditions. VAAIW represents another layer of violence against Indigenous People that requires multidimensional and parallel responses to the structural roots of domination.

# Shortcomings of Research on Violence and Abuse against Women (VAAW)

Although the literature base on violence and abuse has increased over the past 20 years, the need for additional research is clear, particularly with Indigenous women and women of color. The limited number of studies undertaken, small samples, methodological issues, and the lack of diversity within samples are problematic. The focus on quantitative studies, the methodological problems common to crisis-based research, including the reliance on unstructured interventions, small convenience samples, and the lack of comparison groups limit the generalizability of these findings from a mainstream research perspective.

The literature is limited in describing culturally based practice approaches utilizing alternative interventions that define outcomes in diverse ways and substantiate the effectiveness of culturally based approaches. These realities pose a challenge for those interested in this field of study that rely on the existing published and peer-re-viewed knowledge base. The concentration of mainstream interventions focused on personal and interpersonal dynamics of women — to the exclusion of practice emphasizing community and/or political action — limit understanding of the role of engagement in social change as a mechanism for women's empowerment. Micro-level approaches focusing exclusively on women too often fail to critique societal forces and attitudes promoting the degradation of women and the multiple forms of violence and oppression directed at women. Too often, micro-level approaches shift attention away from experiences of colonization and conditions of oppression and reinforce deficit approaches and women-blaming approaches, effectively maintaining the status quo. Until the view is broadened, the multidimensional nature of violence-based oppression will not be effectively challenged or changed by those who rely on the existing knowledge, as these issues are often conspicuously absent from the discussion.

These issues become glaringly evident when considering underserved populations, such as First Nations women. There is a limited base of literature documenting the level of violence and abuse for Indigenous women. There is a gap in research examining whether Indigenous women who experience violence or abuse are statistically different from Indigenous women. There is inadequate research to support empowerment-based frameworks, or other frameworks, as best practice for working with Indigenous women. Rigorous examination of colonization, structural disruption, and the relationship to existing social conditions facing Indigenous People today are either fully absent or only briefly touched upon in disciplines in which one would expect such critiques to occur, including the curriculum of social work programs.

Despite these shortcomings, existing research on intimate partner violence has initiated systematic examination of commonly held assumptions and philosophic orientations about violence. It has contributed to understandings about violence in the lives of women and raised awareness and interest of emerging scholars in the examination of these issues. These achievements have been attained using different approaches and perspectives that further advance the work occurring.

# Social Work and Empowerment Practice

Given the history of colonialism and colonization and the multi-dimensional effects on Indigenous Nations, it is imperative for social workers and others interested in social justice to be versed in the language of decolonization, including *capacity-building, sovereignty,* and *self-determination* to provide effective and culturally relevant practice and advocacy. Such work cannot occur without questioning the influence of historical and contemporary social policies and practices that are often the source of social problems and focus of oppressed groups seeking meaningful and long-term structural change.

Critical analysis skills that integrate analysis of oppression are important to the processes that can be used in empowerment-based strategies, approaches, and practice. Consciousness of the structural issues that have contributed to the colonization of gender for First Nations women is a necessary step in such practice. Culturally competent practice, as reflected in the social work literature, suggests the need for critical consciousness of at least three criteria for such practice:

1) Recognition of the diversity of cultures and the effects of such on the individual, family, and community;

2) Awareness of the strengths that exist in the unique cultures, social structures, and experiences of Indigenous People; and

3) Knowledge of the context of the experiences that have shaped the lives of those worked with, as well as the issues and challenges manifested by these experiences.[56]

Since the 1960s, social workers committed to ideas of social reform and radical social work practice have challenged the structures of domination and the power relationships within these systems and advocated for liberation for a host of groups and social movements, including women and the Women's Movement. In order to challenge and change structures that oppress, understanding the nature of power and the role of social work and other institutions

---

56. Brave Heart & DeBruyn (1998); Lowery (1998); Weaver & Brave Heart (1999); Yellow Bird & Chenault (1999).

of social control are essential underpinnings of social work practice. Models of social work practice that focus on stability and preserving the status quo fail to challenge class, gender, race, and other forms of oppression based on social, economic, and political arrangements, and, as such, have little to offer in the work of Indigenous decolonization. Engaging in social work practice framed by a knowledge base that forces examination of issues of gender, ethnicity, and class, as well as racism, sexism, and poverty is central to social justice practice and equally relevant to progressive and action-oriented disciplines, outside of social work.

Given the context of colonization and oppression affecting First Nations People, particularly Indigenous women, the need for empowerment-oriented advocacy, intervention, and practice would seem evident. First Nations women, engaged in the exercise of their power, seeking to gain control and to resist neo-colonialism should not be further victimized by approaches that fail to recognize the interpersonal and structural dynamics that contribute to conditions of subjugation. *Empowerment practice* is one of the approaches that easily incorporates such approaches. Empowerment processes engage social workers in activities *with* those served to reduce the powerlessness created in systems, structures, and processes that assign negative valuations to marginalized groups. Empowerment-oriented social work practice maintains that the knowledge and skills provided should facilitate personal, interpersonal, and political power.[57] This body of scholarship challenges practitioners to examine the range of interpersonal, and structural issues blocking the growth, development, and functioning of those they work with, as well as those engaged in these efforts, including social workers. The analysis of policies and power dynamics that support oppression and perpetuate inequity is not a theoretical exercise, but instead preparation for engaging with individuals, groups, and communities in sociopolitical action to change oppressive and disempowering social conditions. As such, these approaches reject victim-blaming or deficit orientations of the past and require structural analysis for long-term change.

---

57. Gutierrez & Ortega (1991).

Empowerment-based frameworks propose assessment and practice strategies that evaluate the interpersonal and structural dynamics of issues facing clients.[58] This framework is especially useful in advancing the concept of Indigenous empowerment for practice with Indigenous women in social work and other disciplines. Considering the significant disruption and effects of colonization on women would appear to have considerable value for First Nations women and others who value the revitalization of traditional knowledge systems, as well as the gendered teachings and practices of Indigenous Peoples.

*Empowerment is a process of gaining control over one's life and the complex factors that contribute to oppression.* While social workers are not responsible for the process of empowerment in a client's life, they are responsible for building on the strengths and power of those for whom they work and are responsible in working for social change and speaking very honestly about the truth. Shifting from deficit-based models to empowerment-based practice by addressing personal and social power and the structures of power in the lives of clients is pivotal to this work. *Empowerment means believing* people are cable of making their own choices and decisions and facilitating processes that enable a person to do so. Social work practice is always political because it challenges existing assumptions and societal structures that disempower people, and the role of the discipline in empowerment is to engage in strategies and practices that seek to eliminate institutionalized oppression and empower those persons versus approaches that dehumanize people.

Overcoming the experience of gender-based disempowerment and oppression is not a spectator event but instead one that requires the active engagement of women in multiple layers of change without reinforcing a paradigm of victimization.[59] Practice approaches that build on the strengths and resilience of First Nations women and the informal networks that have sustained these communities in the face of overwhelming odds are crucial to practice

---

58. Lee (2001).
59. Hooks (1995).

based on empowernst. Approaches cognizant of the multiple layers of oppression in the lives of Indigenous women and that validate the strengths and resiliency of Indigenous women while acknowledging and addressing the historic turbulence encountered are important strategies in the work of Indigenous decolonization. The utilization of models and theoretical perspectives that do the same are equally important. Such approaches are essential in understanding context and the multiple layers of work that exists in the lives of those who have been oppressed historically and currently, and such approaches require engagement with the strengths, resources, and capacity within tribal communities.

The root of many current social and health problems among First Nations people were seeded in colonialism, fertilized by colonization, and birthed into systems of White, male-based power structures. Specific, deliberate, and ongoing attempts have been made and continue to be made to destroy Indigenous people, physically, culturally, economically, politically, and spiritually. Tremendous damage to individual, families, and communities has occurred, and the trauma experience has not healed or been fully acknowledged on a societal basis.

# Social Policies That Promote Oppression or Empowerment

A strengths-based empowerment framework was used as the basis for engaging in critical analysis of the Violence Against Women Act (VAWA).[60] This framework uses criteria consistent with the strengths and empowerment perspectives in determining the adequacy, efficiency, and equity of social policy, such as VAWA for Indigenous women. Examination of social policy provides important

---

60. Violence Against Women Act (VAWA) (1994); Violence Against Women Act (VAWA) — Victims of Trafficking and Violence Protection Act (2000); Violence Against Women and Department of Justice Reauthorization Act (2005).

insight into the extent to which policies promote oppression or empowerment.

The VAWA is described as the most extensive support ever given by the federal government to improving, expanding, and enhancing services to battered women.[61] VAWA was originally enacted as Title IV of the Violence Crime Control and Law Enforcement Act of 1994, P.L.103-322.[62] This legislation addresses the physical and sexual assault of women by strengthening current laws and reporting requirements and by providing education on the dynamics of violence to those within these systems. The primary focus of VAWA is centered on stronger criminal penalties for male perpetrators and restitution for women victims *after* violence has occurred.[63]

Chapter two of this legislation describes the responsibility of the federal government to fund law enforcement and prosecution grants for state governments and Indian tribal governments. The legislation requires grantees to distribute 25% of STOP grant funds,[64] the primary funding mechanism, to each of the following areas: victim services, law enforcement, prosecution, and discretionary funding. In fiscal year 1995, STOP grant awards totaled $23.5 million to states through formula grants and $1 million to tribal governments for the development of victim services program to prevent and respond to domestic violence in First Nations country. Between 1995 and 2000, 123 tribal governments received funding under this Act, designated as *STOP (Service-Training-Officers-Prosecutors) Grant Programs for Reducing Violence Against Indian Women*, or *STOP grants*.[65]

To receive STOP grants, recipients are required to implement a series of legislative and policy changes in law enforcement, prosecution, and victim services that reduce the burden on women and improve responses to women subjected to violence and abuse. Funds

---

61. Meyer-Emerick (2001); Roche & Sadoski (1996).

62. Violence Against Women Act (VAWA) (1994).

63. Meyer-Emerick (2001).

64. United States Department of Justice, Office of Violence Against Women (n.d.).

65. Luna, Ferguson, Williams, Jr., et al. (2002).

are used for activities such as training law enforcement personnel and prosecutors on domestic violence, hiring staff for victim services programs, expanding free legal services for the preparation of protection orders, and creating multidisciplinary teams to respond to domestic violence and sexual assault.[66]

# Violence and Abuse against Women (VAAW) and First Nations Peoples

The unique political status of First Nations People in the United States establishes specific legal rights for Indigenous People and responsibilities between tribal governments and the federal government that have historically influenced social policy development and implementation. This complex cultural, political, and legal relationship is important in understanding the response of the federal government to tribal peoples, as well as the response of tribes to pressing social issues, such as VAAW.[67] While the infusion of revenues from STOP grants has produced benefits in tribal communities, debates are also increasing about the effects of these grants in eroding the sovereign rights of tribal governments.[68] These issues will be addressed within the broad social policy analysis of VAWA and the funding mechanism for VAWA initiatives and STOP grants.

## Adequacy

The successful transformation of the issue of VAAIW into a legislative and funding priority is based on a problem-centered orientation that largely overlooks the role of colonization or the structural dynamics of oppression in First Nations communities. The language of federal law, as it relates to violence and abuse, is con-

---

66. Luna, Ferguson, Williams, Jr., et al. (2002); Meyer-Emerick (2001); National Institute of Justice (2000).

67. Luna, Ferguson, Williams, Jr., et al. (2002).

68. United States Department of Justice, Office of Violence Against Women (n.d.).

sistent with past practices that utilize a pathology orientation in social policy formulation.[69] The VAAW emphasizes responses of law enforcement and criminal justice systems to violence and abuse and ignores the need to address larger structural conditions that support the denigration and violent oppression of women. In this approach, the violence against Indigenous women is transformed into an attack on the state. The reliance on the criminal justice system and the funding priorities dedicated to law enforcement and prosecution in VAWA, while tough on crime, are inadequate responses for addressing VAAW. It is well documented that women of color oppressed by violence and abuse are frequently re-victimized by the criminal justice systems and are too often blamed for becoming victims.[70] Centering the responses to VAAW in the criminal justice system can strain the relationship between criminal justice and victim services and the often adversarial theoretical orientations that exist within each, particularly when sentencing disparities exist for tribal men who have perpetrated violence against Indigenous women versus their non-tribal counterparts.

## Efficacy

Reservation-based programs have been the primary recipients of VAIW STOP grants due to language within the legislation that limit eligibility to federally recognized Indian tribal governments. This wording is intended to recognize the government-to-government relations between tribal government and the federal government. As sovereigns, tribal governments can partner with or subcontract with non-government agencies, including off-reservation non-profit programs. STOP grants provide desperately needed resources to tribal communities devastated by policies of colonization, including VAAIW. However, an estimated two-thirds of all Indigenous women live in urban areas and, because they do not reside on reservation, off-reservation programs are effectively excluded from STOP grant eligibility. Tribal women living in urban

---

69. Chapin (1994).
70. INCITE & Mantilla (2002); Meyer-Emerick (2001); Smith (2000).

areas with substantial Indigenous populations report an absence of culturally based victim-service programs because these programs are ineligible for STOP grant funding.[71] Urban programs may request a limited stream of discretionary funding; however, this funding is based on the condition that services are also provided to adjoining reservation communities. Off-reservation programs may also apply for STOP grants made available to state government. Such requirements are inefficient in addressing the unique demographic and cultural needs of urban women isolated from reservation communities who experience violence and abuse.

The emphasis of tribal STOP grants has been on developing coordinated community responses to violence against Indian women that emphasize networking and the establishment of working agreements between various stakeholder groups, that is, criminal justice and victim services.[72] In the area of victim services, STOP grants have been used:

- to overcome jurisdictional issues that delay protection orders;
- to establish sanctions for violations of these orders within tribal court systems;
- to train specialized domestic violence advocates;
- to provide community training to law enforcement, prosecutors, and community members on domestic violence;
- to develop shelters and safe houses; and
- to establish telephone hotlines, supports groups, crisis intervention services, and referral services.

STOP grants have generated resources for tribes to strengthen and develop criminal justice and prosecution systems, as well as the infrastructures and supports needed to operate these structures. As "self-governing entities in the U.S. legal system, able to make and enforce a variety of laws in Indian country"[73] tribes have the right not only to determine how social problems will be addressed, but

---

71. Personal observation in 2002 based on conversations with tribal women in Albuquerque, NM, and Lawrence, KS.
72. Luna, Ferguson, Williams, Jr., et al. (2002).
73. Luna, Ferguson, Williams, Jr., et al. (2002, p. 36).

also, and perhaps more importantly, to determine how tribal judicial and legal systems are structured and the models on which social systems are based.

Upon closer examination, social policy, such as VAWA, effectively undermines this right of tribal self-determination by imposing conditions for "acceptable" responses and "foreign" criminal justice systems on tribal communities. Tribal systems of justice must meet the broad categories of law enforcement and prosecution, as defined by the mainstream legal system in order to qualify for STOP grants. Such practices divert resources away from the problem of violence, as understood and defined by tribal peoples, to creating acceptable criminal justice and victim service systems evaluated by Western standards. This effectively maintains the status quo and engages tribal people to conspire in cultural self-annihilation by marginalizing traditional Indigenous systems of restorative justice.

While there are legitimate jurisdictional issues and a broad array of tribal codes and ordinances related to violence against Indigenous women that must often be negotiated, too often solutions to the complexity of issues assume funding to support the implementation of adversarial mainstream legal systems will solve the problem. Such strategies fail to consider the further erosion of sovereignty, as well as the traditional and culturally based systems of justice and healing within tribal communities when funding is premised on the superiority of mainstream practices, approaches, and systems.

## Equity

The reliance on federal and private sources of funding that requires submission to institutionalized pathological and deficit-based models in order to *qualify* for the help needed is problematic for Indigenous Peoples on several levels. Because the funding for STOP grants for tribal programs are limited to reservation-based programs, the approach suggests that tribal men in reservation communities are the sole perpetrators of violence against and abuse against Indigenous women. This reinforces stereotypes and further pathologizes First Nations men and communities, both on and off-reservation. The author recognizes violence and abuse occurs in tribal communities; however, reports by the United States Department of Justice[74] and the *National Violence Against Women Survey*[75] suggest tribal women, in urban and reservation settings, may be at a greater risk for a spectrum of violence and abuse from non-tribal men. The high rates of intermarriage and urbanization of Indigenous People suggest the need to evaluate the violence and abuse being experienced by First Nations women, particularly that perpetrated by non-tribal men in urban settings and relationships. First Nations People have remarkably high rates of intermarriage compared with other racial groups: 53% are married to non-Indigenous people, with 48% of Indigenous women married to White men.[76] Urban First Nations women are not immune from violence and abuse. Instead, funding for culturally appropriate services addressing the unique needs of Indigenous urban women has been neglected.

Additionally, in a 1978 landmark legal case, Oliphant v. Suquamish Indian Tribe,[77] the Supreme Court ruled that tribes lack jurisdiction over non-Indians unless Congress has expressly given it that power. Because non-Indigenous perpetrators were effectively immune from criminal prosecution by tribes for VAAIW, these perpetrators of VAAIW are immune from prosecution on reservations. In comparison, Indigenous men who commit VAAIW, are potentially subject to be simultaneously tried and sentenced under tribal, state, and federal laws, including the Major Crimes Act of 1885.[78] This Act authorizes federal officials to prosecute tribal men who are reservation residents under stiffer federal statutes, creating a disparity in sentencing. Clearly, the development of policy should be strongly influenced by those affected to avoid ineffective policymaking and doing greater harm to vulnerable populations. The need for provisions addressing and responding to the spectrum of

---

74. United States Department of Justice (1999).
75. Tjaden & Thoennes (1998; 1999).
76. Yellow Bird & Snipp (1994).
77. Oliphant v. Suquamish Indian Tribe (1978).
78. Major Crimes Act (1885).

violence and abuse faced by First Nations women, regardless of geographic residency, is important.

The emphasis on interdisciplinary approaches to violence and abuse that address the need for prevention and education across society are also lacking within the current policy and require attention. Finally, policies that forces imposition of foreign systems upon another culture are reminiscent of imperialistic policies of oppression. Promoting culturally sensitive responses and policies while systematically dismantling Indigenous social systems and defining the problem for First Nations People does little to empower and more to oppress Indigenous people and communities. Perhaps most concerning is the blatant potential for disparity in justice for Indigenous perpetrators and non-tribal perpetrators.

# Chapter Five

# Empowerment as a Paradigm for Inquiry

*Indigenous Nations are the most studied and least understood Peoples in the United States* (Chenault, 2003, personal communication).

Research studies are one of the mechanisms useful in answering questions about issues such as violence and abuse against Indigenous women (VAAIW). Within higher education, such studies are often undertaken by students pursuing doctoral degrees and faculty who are competing for tenure within these institutions. This section describes the methodology and findings of the only doctoral research study on VAAIW, which was completed in 2004.[1] A modified study was replicated in a second population of Indigenous women in 2009 by this author,[2] and the results demonstrate similar alarming prevalence and incidence rates of violence and abuse in a sample of urban Indigenous women in a central plains tribe.

The original goal of the 2004 study[3] was to generate information for the improvement of policy and practice in the field of violence and abuse and to generate data-driven research useful for tribal governments and programs addressing VAAIW. There was a desire to understand whether younger tribal women were experiencing less violence and abuse than older tribal women. After all,

---

1. Chenault (2004).
2. Chenault (2009, unpublished data on violence and abuse findings for Prairie Band Potawatomi Women).
3. Chenault (2004).

several decades of work by the Women's Movement had occurred, and it made sense that less violence and abuse would be reported. There was also in interest in understanding whether VAAIW affected the power of women; thus, constructs from social work associated with empowerment (self-esteem, social support/sense of belonging, and social action) were used to operationalize empowerment. Using a modified subscale of the *National Violence Against Women Survey*,[4] this research collected data in on the prevalence and incidence of VAAIW a population of college women that were useful for the purposes of establishing a baseline for the existence of violence and abuse.

Various stakeholder groups representing Indigenous women and First Nations People were consulted formally and informally throughout the process. Recommendations and feedback were solicited on the topic, the research design, and the empowerment framework advanced for the study. These processes were intended to provide voice to First Nations women and tribal programs whose contributions have been marginalized by academy, an element of participatory or community-based research that is reflective of empowerment practice. These contributions were used in the construction of survey questions, particularly when tribal women consistently questioned findings in national studies. In numerous settings, this type of feedback was received about a United States Department of Justice study reporting the majority of perpetrators (70%) of VAAIW were White males.[5] Consistently, Indigenous women indicated that tribal men were more likely to engage in violence and abuse in their experience. It was important to include an item on the race of the perpetrator to explore this question and others raised by tribal women.

---

4. Tjaden & Thoennes (1998; 1999).
5. United States Department of Justice (1999); United States Department of Justice & Perry (2004).

# Research Question

Two primary questions were considered in the 2004 study:[6]

1) *What is the lifetime prevalence and incidence of violence and abuse in a college sample of tribal women?*

2) *Do significant group differences for four variables (self-esteem, social support, sense of belonging, and social action) associated with empowerment exist between First Nations college women who have experienced violence and abuse and those who have not experienced violence and abuse?*

Regarding the first question, *prevalence* refers to *the percentage of people within a demographic group experiencing the phenomenon during a specific period*; *incidence* describes *the number of separate incidents within a group during a specific period.*[7] The second question considered in this study was whether significant group differences on four variables (self-esteem, social support, sense of belonging, and social action) associated with empowerment existed between First Nations college women who have experienced violence and abuse and those who have not experienced violence and abuse. It was hypothesized that Indigenous women who experienced violence and abuse would report lower scores on these variables.

The research questions posed could have been evaluated using a quantitative, qualitative, or mixed method design. A quantitative design was consistent with the existing research and provided an opportunity to address gaps in the literature on empowerment research. As discussed by prior researchers, the failure to carefully define the concepts of empowerment for research purposes has diminished academic respect for the value of empowerment approaches generally.[8]

Given the overall importance of empowerment to the full examination of VAAIW, the merits of qualitative research were equally supportable as these approaches ensure that the voice of women

---

6. Chenault (2004).
7. Tjaden & Thoennes (1998; 1999).
8. Freeman (2001).

oppressed by violence is at the forefront of the examination. The subjugation of the knowledge and experiences of populations who have been disempowered by a marginal status in the social order and disenfranchised by the lack of meaningful participation in the academy, as well as in the decision-making processes, readily substantiated the case for research methods to ensure meaningful opportunities for voice and the acknowledgement of strengths. Qualitative research, with its core philosophies immersed in the wisdom of the experience, provided a compelling alternative to research soundly castigated as a tool of privilege. All marginal groups in this society who suffer grave injustices, who are victimized by institutionalized systems of domination (e.g., race, class, gender), are faced with the peculiar dilemma of developing strategies that draw attention to one's plight in a way that will merit regard and consideration without re-inscribing a paradigm of victimization.[9] While a qualitative design was plausible, such a design did not readily fit the need to establish the scope of the problem or a baseline for prevalence and incidence reporting. A quantitative design provided the opportunity to advance the importance of the issue and to create change by providing prevalence and incidence data to establish a starting point for change. In order to establish a baseline study of prevalence and incidence rates and to advance measurable variables of empowerment, a quantitative design was selected. Ensuring that meaningful dialogue occurred in the processes leading up to the study may effectively mitigate the frequently identified limits of quantitative research.

# Empowerment as a
# Paradigm for Inquiry

One of the most significant research challenges for the evaluation of empowerment practice is associated with the *conceptualization* into measurable outcomes useful for empirical study.

---

9. Hooks (1995).

Freeman[10] maintains that empowerment literature has tended to differentiate empowerment in terms of being a set of characteristics existing within systems, particular processes used, practice or research strategies employed, a type of desired outcomes, or some combination of these factors. For the purpose of this study, *empowerment* was approached as *a set of characteristics present at various levels—personal, interpersonal, and community or political— that can be altered or reduced as a result of experiences such as violence and abuse.* Empowerment is manifested by particular indicators at each of these levels, such as self-esteem, social support, sense of belonging, and social action. The 2004 study[11] was an exploratory study intended to generate insight into whether these constructs for evaluating empowerment in Indigenous communities are culturally relevant or significant. Empowerment is not only self-esteem or social support, but also the changes in perceptions, attitudes, knowledge, skills, or social action that results from the changes one makes to become liberated from multiple levels of oppression. Taking back power that has been given away, coerced, or taken away and using that power to effect change in multiple areas of one's life exemplify empowerment.

Empowerment cannot be achieved by focusing solely on personal dimensions (*self-esteem*) to the exclusion of the interpersonal dimension (*social support*) or community dimension (*social action*) but instead is interconnected with each of the dimensions. The intent of this study was to examine *selected* variables associated with empowerment and to test differences in these variables between women who experienced violence or abuse and women who had not experience violence or abuse.

As discussed previously, the approach to this study integrated elements of participatory action research emphasizing the development of critical consciousness, improvement of the lives of tribal women, and the need for social change[12] by involvement of First Nations women and communities in the research process and

10. Freeman (2001).
11. Chenault (2004).
12. Glesne & Peshkin (1992); Maguire (1987).

through selection of theoretical frameworks responsive to structural and power dynamics. The reflections of these stakeholders influenced the overall research process, confirming the need for this study, but also validating the importance of traditional knowledge about tribal women and approaches that integrate tribal worldviews into the responses to violence and abuse. A conscious effort was made to identify tribally based programs responding to the issues of VAAIW and making personal contact with key individuals in these organizations, visiting the project, or obtaining materials about the approaches used in the program. An effort was also made to weave the practice wisdom of culturally based and innovative Indigenous approaches into the empowerment constructs and questions used in the survey. While this study is the only study focusing on VAAIW that uses a national tribally diverse sample of Indigenous college women, a tremendous amount remains to be understood.

# Definitions of Key Concepts

*Empowerment* describes *simultaneous and multiple levels of change that build on the unique strengths, resources, and capacities of individuals, groups, and communities to challenge and overcome oppressive practices and systems at the micro, mezzo, and macro levels.*

*Self-Esteem* is defined as *the feeling of satisfaction a person has about self.* Self-esteem was identified in the literature as a trait diminished by multiple forms of subjugation, including gender and cultural oppression.[13] Self-esteem was measured by using the Rosenberg Self-Esteem Scale,[14] the most common survey identified in this field.

*Social Support* and a *Sense of Belonging* were measured using two subscales from the Interpersonal Support and Evaluation List.[15]

---

13. Tutty, Bidgood & Rothery (1993); Walters (1999).
14. Rosenberg (1989).
15. Cohen & Hoberman (1983). The scale is available at: http://www.psy.cmu.edu/~scohen/ISEL.html.

- The *social support* subscale measured the perceived *availability of someone to talk to.*
- The *sense-of-belonging* subscale measured the perceived *availability of someone to do things with.*

A sense of belonging and social support function as buffers in protecting one from the pathogenic effects of high levels of stress predictive of depression and psychological problems. A modified version of the Interpersonal Support and Evaluation List, containing 21 statements about sense of belonging and social support, with higher scores indicating greater support and belonging, was used to determine the level of social support and sense of belonging in the study population.

*Social Action* was measured using two questions related to participation or involvement in activities consistent with the *third dimension of empowerment: community and/or political involvement.* These two questions contained multiple possible responses.

In the first question, participants were queried about their participation in cultural activities and asked to mark all responses that apply. The responses included:

- Participation in traditional cultural ceremonies or activities;
- Participation in women's cultural activities, such as talking circles; or
- Participation in healing practices or ceremonies, such as sweat lodges.

Participation in spiritual, political, and cultural activities or social action that seeks to educate tribal people and to renew or preserve cultural traditions is associated with positive cultural identity and psychological wellness.[16]

The second primary question explored participation in activities promoting positive social change in tribal communities, using the instruction to "mark all that apply." Participants could select items that included:

---

16. Walters (1999).

- Participation in/or supporting activities that promote social change in tribal communities;
- Participation in education about violence and abuse against women (VAAW); and
- Participation in activities seeking to change laws, policies, or programs for women who have experienced violence and abuse.

Responses were subsequently transformed into a new single variable, *social action*, which describes *participation in activities in tribal communities that promote social action or social change*, constructs consistent with the third dimension of empowerment (community/political involvement).

# Study Results

Detailed discussion of the statistical analyses used in this study is intentionally limited to reach a broad and general audience of readers with an interest in this topic. Descriptive statistics for the sample and statistically significant findings will be discussed in this section. Data were collected and analyzed using univariate, bivariate, and multivariate analysis, including independent samples *t* tests, correlation analysis, analysis of variance, and reliability analysis.[17]

## Sample

The participants in the 2004 study[18] were 112 Indigenous female students attending a small tribal college in the central plains. The sample size represented 23% of the female students enrolled at the college. All female students (492) received a flyer through campus mail inviting participation in this study. Flyers were also posted throughout campus prior to the project inviting student partici-

---

17. Chenault (2004) provides detailed information on statistical findings from this study.
18. Chenault (2004).

pation with particular emphasis on placing flyers in high-traffic areas and on the inside door of bathroom stalls. Requirements for approval of human subjects research were met at the tribal college and the University of Kansas (Lawrence, KS). On the scheduled date of the survey, women came to the survey location where they were greeted and the survey process was explained. Each participant received a consent form and completed a self-administered questionnaire in a large centrally located conference room on campus. Participants were able to come at their convenience and surveys were completed throughout the day. Each survey was completed at one sitting and every student who came to the location completed the questionnaire and the consent form. After completion of the survey and consent form, each participant was given a resource list of local agencies providing services to women who have experienced violence or abuse and asked to either post the flyer or pass it on to someone who might need the information, if the participant did not need the information.

## Measures

A survey packet was developed for the collection of demographic information, as well as for measuring differences in the dependent variables, self-esteem, social support, sense of belonging, and social action. These dependent variables were initially identified from the existing research literature on VAAW and then categorized into one of the three dimensions of empowerment: personal, interpersonal, and community/political spheres. Standardized measures for self-esteem, social support, and sense of belonging, including the modified Rosenberg Self-Esteem Scale[19] and the Interpersonal Support and Evaluation List,[20] both of which have had limited use with First Nations women and in research on VAAW. This study proposed a theoretical model that explored differences between the independent variables — those who experience violence or abuse

---

19. Rosenberg (1989).

20. Cohen & Hoberman (1983). The scale is available at: http://www.psy.cmu.edu/~scohen/ISEL.html.

and those who do not — on the four dependent variables associated with empowerment: self-esteem, social support, sense of belonging, and community/political action.

## Demographic Profile

Table 5.1 summarizes the demographic profile of the study participants. The women in this study ranged in age from 18 to 53 years, with an average age of 25.72 years. Most respondents were age 18 to 25 years (66.9%). The next largest age group of respondents was age 26 to 30 years (17.9%), followed by the age group of 31 to 53 years

Table 5.1  Demographic Profile ($N = 112$)

| Variable ($N$) | Frequency ($n$) | Percent (%) |
|---|---|---|
| **Age** (M = 25.72) | | |
| 18–24 | 68 | 60.7 |
| 25–30 | 27 | 24.1 |
| 31–40 | 8 | 7.0 |
| 41–53 | 9 | 8.0 |
| **Income** (109) | | |
| <$5,000 | 25 | 22.9 |
| $5,001–10,000 | 30 | 27.5 |
| $10,001–15,000 | 12 | 11.0 |
| >$15,001 | 42 | 38.5 |
| **Marital Status** (111) | | |
| Married | 7 | 6.3 |
| Living with someone | 14 | 12.5 |
| Single, never married | 75 | 67.0 |
| Divorced | 14 | 12.5 |
| Separated | 1 | 0.9 |
| **Student Classification** (112) | | |
| Freshman | 41 | 36.6 |
| Sophomore | 37 | 33.0 |
| Junior | 18 | 16.1 |
| Senior | 16 | 14.3 |
| **Children** (112) | | |
| Yes | 35 | 31.3 |
| No | 77 | 68.8 |

(15.1%). Recent studies on tribal colleges report that the average age of these college students is dropping from an earlier report of age 27 years, which reflects the "second generation" trend, resulting in larger numbers of younger students attending tribal colleges.[21]

Most of the participants were freshmen (36.6%) or sophomores (33.0%); 16.1% were juniors, and 14.3% were seniors. This tribal college began offering baccalaureate degrees in 1998 and the numbers for juniors and seniors was consistent with the enrollment patterns: 13% of students were classified as juniors and 9% as seniors. More than two-thirds (67%) were single, and 68.8% reported having no children. In the past, most tribal college students were older and female, often with children.[22] All of the participants were enrolled members of federally recognized tribes and corporations, which makes this sample very unique.

## Cultural Profile

Table 5.2 summarizes the tribal affiliations of the study participants. The cultural profile of the study sample is presented in **Table 5.3**, which encompasses the degree of indigenous blood, primary cultural influence, involvement in cultural activities, and involvement in social action. This sample provides insight into the diversity of tribal affiliation and levels of cultural participation, as well as the shifting demographics present among First Nations women. In the sample of 112 participants, 100% of the sample members were enrolled members of federally recognized tribes, representing 39 culturally distinct Indigenous Nations. The degree of Indian blood required for enrollment varies among tribes and increasingly reflects affiliation in more than one tribal group and/or cultural or ethnic groups. This diversity is reflected in the reported degree of tribal blood identified by the 112 participants:

- 31.3% — reported being full-blood tribal members;
- 14.3% — at least three-quarters but not full-blood;

---

21. Boyer & Boyer (1997).
22. Ibid.

## Table 5.2  Tribal Affiliations of Participants*

| Indigenous Nation | |
|---|---|
| Apache | Meskwaki |
| Athabascan | Ojibwa |
| Caddo | Omaha |
| Cherokee | Osage |
| Cheyenne | Paiute |
| Chippewa | Ponca |
| Choctaw | Potawatomi |
| Creek | Pueblo |
| Crow | Sac and Fox |
| Dine | Seminole |
| Eskimo | Seneca |
| Gros Ventre | Shoshone |
| Havasupai | Sioux |
| Hoopa Valley | Three Affiliated Tribes |
| Indigenous | (Mandan, Hidatsa, and Arikara) |
| Iowa | Tohono O'odham |
| Kaw | Tonkawa |
| Kickapoo | Ute |
| Klamath | Winnebago |
| Lakota | Yakima |

* Represents 26% of tribes at the college based on responses of study participants.

- 21.4%—at least one-half but less than three-quarters;
- 18.8%—more than one-quarter but less than one-half; and
- 10.7%—less than one-quarter.

Each federally recognized tribe in the United States establishes its own criteria for determining membership eligibility. *Blood quantum* is the most widely used criteria for enrollment, with *degree of blood determined from parents and ancestors* and their *blood quantum as determined by tribal census rolls.*

Approximately 50% of the participants (44.6%) reported their primary cultural influence was a combination of mainstream and tribal culture, with more mainstream influence. Approximately 50% were raised in a city or urban area (49.1%), with approximately 33% (31.3%) being raised on a reservation, tribal land,

## Table 5.3  Cultural Profile of Sample ($N = 112$)

| Variable | Frequency ($n$) | Percent (%) |
|---|---|---|
| **Degree of Indigenous Blood**[1] | | |
| Less than one-quarter (<1/4) | 12 | 10.7 |
| More than one-quarter but less than one-half (>1/4–1/2) | 21 | 18.8 |
| At least one-half but less than three-quarters (≥1/2–<3/4) | 24 | 21.4 |
| At least three-quarters but not full-blood (≥3/4–<4/4) | 16 | 14.3 |
| Full blood (4/4) | 35 | 31.3 |
| Unknown | 4 | 3.6 |
| **Primary Cultural Influence** | | |
| Mainstream culture | 20 | 17.9 |
| Tribal culture | 12 | 10.7 |
| Combination, more mainstream | 50 | 44.6 |
| Combination, more tribal | 25 | 22.3 |
| None of the above | 5 | 4.5 |
| **Where Primarily Raised?**[2] | | |
| City or urban area | 55 | 49.1 |
| Reservation, tribal land, pueblo or village | 35 | 31.3 |
| Rural area, not reservation | 20 | 17.9 |
| None of the above | 2 | 1.8 |
| **Involvement in Cultural Activities** | | |
| None of the above | 29 | 25.9 |
| One activity | 36 | 32.1 |
| Two activities | 30 | 26.8 |
| Three activities | 17 | 15.2 |
| **Involvement in Social Action** | | |
| None of the above | 64 | 57.1 |
| One activity | 30 | 26.8 |
| Two activities | 11 | 9.8 |
| Three activities | 7 | 6.3 |

1. Note that each federally recognized tribe in the United States establishes its own criteria for determining membership eligibility. Blood quantum is the most widely used criteria for enrollment, with degree of blood determined from parents and ancestors and their blood quantum as determined by tribal census rolls.

2. Note that the profile point, "Where primarily raised?" refers to the primary geographic location during childhood.

pueblo, or village, a trend also reflected in the 2000 United States Census Bureau data.[23]

## Prevalence and Incidence of Violence and Abuse

First Nations women have been identified as experiencing a range of violence and abuse, including the experiences of violent crimes such as rape and physical assault, intimate partner violence, which may include emotional abuse, and being threatened or stalked, as presented in **Table 5.4**. Indigenous women are not only confronted with a gamut of violence and abuse experiences, but also this population experiences disproportionate levels of violence and abuse, within family systems, as well as in the larger community and society.

Findings from this study corroborated the global nature of violence and abuse experienced by Indigenous women, as well as the disproportionate levels of violence and abuse in this population of First Nations college students. The overwhelming majority of this sample (85.7%) reported having experienced at least one form of violence and abuse in their lifetime compared with those who had no experience of violence and abuse (14.2%). The most common form of violence and abuse was identified as emotional abuse (75.9%), followed by physical victimization (66%), sexual victimization (35.7%), being threatened (27.7%), and being stalked (26.8%).

Table 5.4  Experiences of Violence and Abuse ($N = 112$)

| Type of Violence and Abuse | Frequency ($n$) | Percent (%) |
| --- | --- | --- |
| Emotional abuse | 85 | 75.9 |
| Physical victimization | 74 | 66.1 |
| Sexual victimization | 40 | 35.7 |
| Threatened | 31 | 27.7 |
| Stalked | 30 | 26.8 |

23. United States Census Bureau (2000).

*Emotional abuse,* also referred to as *verbal abuse* or *psychological abuse,* is delineated by a *range of behaviors that do not involve physical force, but that establish dominance and control over an individual through tactics such as intimidation, belittling, or subordination, and diminish one's belief in self.*[24] In this study, emotional abuse was characterized as being putdown, yelled at, or made to feel inadequate. While emotional abuse may intersect with other forms of violence and abuse, it often occurs in the absence of other types of violence. The wounds of emotional abuse can be equally devastating compared with other forms of violence and abuse.

The prevalence and incidence rates of physical and sexual violence in this study are similar to the tribal clinic studies of Indigenous women previously discussed. One of the difficulties with comparing prevalence and incidence rates in various studies are the differences in definitions used, as is the case when *intimate-partner violence* is defined as *combined physical or sexual abuse by current or former spouses, or intimate partners.* Rates of stalking reported in other studies indicate Indigenous women report significantly more stalking than do women of other ethnic/racial backgrounds.[25] In this college study,[26] 27% of the sample reported disproportionate rates of stalking as compared with women nationally. Prevalence rates reported in the *National Violence Against Women Survey* estimate 8% to 12% of women are stalked nationally.[27]

The prevalence of reported violence and abuse across the lifetime of this college sample[28] was equally alarming, as shown in **Table 5.5.** Participants reported multiple experiences of violence and abuse across the lifespan, with 40.6% reporting childhood experiences, 48.9% reporting adolescent experiences, and 73.9% reporting adult experiences of violence and abuse.

---

24. Mouradian (2004); Shepard & Campbell (1992); Smith & Loring (1994).
25. Wallace, Calhoun, Powell, et al. (1996).
26. Chenault (2004).
27. Tjaden & Thoennes (1998; 1999).
28. Chenault (2004).

Table 5.5  Lifetime Experiences of Violence and Abuse ($N = 96$)

| Age at Violence and Abuse (yrs) | Frequency ($n$) | Percent (%) |
|---|---|---|
| Childhood (0–9) | 39 | 40.6 |
| Adolescence (10–16) | 47 | 48.9 |
| Adult ($\geq$17) | 71 | 73.9 |

In order to determine incidence levels of violence and abuse for the past year, participants were asked to identify whether they had experienced violence and abuse over the past 12 months. The majority had not experienced violence and abuse over the past year (58.3%), although a significant number (30.2%) did report violence and abuse experiences, with 13.5% reporting they did not know how many times violence and abuse had occurred during this time frame, perhaps suggesting a larger percentage of past-year violence and abuse (43.7%) than is reported. Because this study involved a tribal college population, items were also included to determine the prevalence of violence and abuse while students at college. A majority of the sample (59.5%) reported no experiences of violence and abuse, 30.8% reported at least one experience of violence and abuse, and an additional 9.6% reported they did not know. Of those participants reporting violence and abuse, 15.9% reported the incident had occurred on campus, 12.7% reported the incident occurred off campus, and 9.5% reported incidents both on and off campus.

The violence and abuse reported by this population of young women mirrors anecdotal reports of violence and abuse by earlier generations of Indigenous women[29] and the first wave of tribal clinic studies on the prevalence and incidence of VAAIW.[30] Young tribal women are experiencing alarming rates of violence and abuse on multiple levels. It is very troubling that 86% of this sample of

---

29. Chapin (1994); Norton & Mason (1995).

30. Bohn (2002); Fairchild, Fairchild, & Stoner (1998); Harwell, Moore, & Spence (2003); Malcoe, Duran, & Montgomery (2004); Robin, Chester, & Rasmussen (1998).

college students, with an average age of 26 years, had been physically victimized, emotionally abused, threatened, stalked, or sexually victimized at least once in their lifetime. Despite attention to issues such as VAAW over the past four decades, violence and abuse against young Indigenous women remains a pressing social issues and cultural aberration that has largely been invisible within helping disciplines such as social work.

# Dynamics of Violence and Abuse against Indigenous Women (VAAIW)

According to the 1999 and 2004 United States Department of Justice reports, *American Indians and Crime*,[31] First Nations victims of rape/sexual assault, violent crimes, and/or intimate and family violence most often reported that the victimization was committed by an offender of a different race, with a majority (60%) of the offenders being identified as White men. The results of this study did not support these findings (**Table 5.6**). Instead, the majority of participants (82.3%) reported the race of the perpetrator as being American Indian, followed by White perpetrators (35.4%), and Black and Hispanic perpetrators (16.7% each), consistent with the feedback received from tribal women in the survey design phase.

Table 5.6  Race/Ethnicity of Perpetrator ($N = 96$)

| Race/Ethnicity | Frequency ($n$) | Percent (%) |
|---|---|---|
| American Indian | 79 | 82.3 |
| White | 34 | 35.4 |
| Black | 16 | 16.7 |
| Hispanic | 16 | 15.7 |
| Asian | 1 | 0.9 |
| Unknown | 5 | 5.0 |

31. United States Department of Justice (1999); United States Department of Justice & Perry (2004).

Table 5.7  Relationship to the Perpetrator of
Violence and Abuse ($N = 96$)

| Relationship to Perpetrator | Frequency ($n$) | Percent (%) |
|---|---|---|
| Boyfriend | 58 | 60.4 |
| Relative(s) | 49 | 51.0 |
| Other | 38 | 39.5 |
| Male live-in roommate | 21 | 22.0 |
| Ex-spouse | 17 | 17.7 |
| Stranger | 17 | 17.7 |
| Female live-in roommate | 7 | 7.0 |
| Current spouse | 5 | 5.0 |

As reported in **Table 5.7**, the experiences of violence and abuse were
not limited to intimate partner violence; instead multiple perpetrators of violence and abuse were identified, including intimate partners, relatives, and strangers. *Intimate-partner violence* is described
as *acts or threats of violence perpetrated by current or former spouses,
intimate partners, or dates.*[32] Although most participants identified
boyfriends or intimate partners as the perpetrators of violence and
abuse most frequently (60.4%), participants also reported disturbing levels of violence and abuse by relatives (51%), violence and
abuse by someone other than a boyfriend, spouse, or relative (39.5%),
a male live-in roommate (22.0%), or ex-spouse (17.7%), as well as
an unsettling level of violence and abuse by strangers (17.7%).

To explore whether existing funding priorities are consistent
with the locations where reported violence and abuse occurred
(urban versus reservation or tribal lands), participants were asked
to identify whether the violence and abuse had occurred in a city
or urban area, on reservation or tribal lands, or in a rural area that
is not on a reservation. **Table 5.8** reports the geographic location
where violence and abuse occurred. Participants reported that most
violence (68.7%) took place in a city or urban area, 30.5% of the
violence and abuse took place on a reservation or tribal land, and
15.7% took place in a rural area not on a reservation. Of note, how-

---

32. Malcoe, Duran, & Montgomery (2004).

Table 5.8  Primary Geographic Location of
Violence and Abuse ($N = 96$)

| Location | Frequency ($n$) | Percent (%) |
|---|---|---|
| City or urban area | 66 | 68.8 |
| Reservation or tribal land | 29 | 30.5 |
| Rural area, not reservation | 15 | 15.7 |
| None of the above | 8 | 8.4 |

ever, the current funding for VAAIW is effectively limited to reservation-based programs.

# Effects of Violence and Abuse

This study also explored participation in cultural activities and the role of traditional practices and ceremonies in the healing process. Practice in tribal settings is increasingly moving toward analysis of colonization and the effects of structural disruption on cultural and gendered teachings. In doing so, these approaches move away from a *pathology orientation* or *deficit orientation* to what has been described as *Indigenous empowerment*. Studies evaluating the effectiveness of these approaches have not been reported in mainstream literature, although they are reported anecdotally.

Participants were asked whether traditional cultural healing practices, such as healing ceremonies, had been used to assist the individual in overcoming violence and abuse. Slightly more than 50% of the participants (51%) reported using at least one traditional healing practice to overcome the incident, while 46.8% reported no use of cultural practices. Within the traditional practices of many tribal communities, *well-being* is not defined purely as a physical phenomenon. Instead *well-being* refers to a more *holistic state that includes the emotional, spiritual, intellectual, and physical dimensions of one's being.* Cultural teachings frequently emphasize maintaining balance in each of these aspects and restoring balance, when needed, using tribally specific healing practices. Indicators of well-being selected from traditional Indigenous cultural and healing practices were explored, including a sense of balance in life, pride, and dignity as a woman, feeling of strength as a woman, participation in cultural activities and connection to other tribal women. Further examination of such items with Indigenous women is needed to refine these constructs in culturally relevant terms.

When asked whether one's sense of balance had been negatively affected, more than 50% (56.8%) reported their sense of balance, or well-being, had been negatively affected. Most participants also reported negative effects on their pride as Indigenous women (53.6%) and their feeling of strength as a woman (57.8%). However, these experiences of violence and abuse did not alienate woman from participation in cultural activities or their connections to other tribal woman, elements that are considered critical in providing a sense of belonging and social support. Most participants reported no negative effects on their participation in cultural activities (87.3%) or in their connections to other tribal women.

The scholarship on empowerment, violence, and abuse recognizes the importance of creating environments in which women who have experienced violence and abuse have meaningful opportunities to have their voices and feelings heard in order to facilitate empowerment.[33] Participants were initially asked too self-identify where they believed they were at in the healing process. Less than 50% (44.7%) reported they had overcome the experience and felt good about where they were in the process, with 32.2% reporting they had worked on the experience and felt better but recognized the need for additional work. There were also participants who reported working on recovery from violence and abuse, but not feeling any better (18.7%) and an additional 5% who reported they had not talked to anyone about their experience.

Participants were asked to respond to eight items rating the effects of violence and abuse on self-esteem, social support, a sense of belonging, and social action. Most women who had experienced violence and abuse reported negative effects on self-esteem (80.1%), and 58.3% reported negative effects on a sense of belonging.

---

33. Shamai (2000).

# Empowerment and Violence and Abuse

A small body of empirical research on VAAW has explored the effects of these experiences on women. Interventions and treatment of women who have experienced violence and abuse typically target outcomes such as self-esteem, social support, sense of belonging, stress and depression levels, or self-efficacy. Table 5.9 presents an empowerment-based framework (personal, interpersonal, community/political spheres) with the targeted variables of self-esteem, sense of belonging and social support, and involvement in cultural and social action activities. Table 5.10 presents an analy-

### Table 5.9  Empowerment-Based Framework and Targeted Variables

| Sphere | Personal | Interpersonal | Community/political |
|---|---|---|---|
| Domain | Self-perception | Knowledge/skills | Action/behaviors |
| Variable | Self-esteem | Sense of belonging and social support | Cultural activities/ social action involvement |

### Table 5.10  Analysis of Variance (ANOVA): Differences between Groups by Empowerment Constructs

| Empowerment Construct | Group | Mean Deviation | Standard | N |
|---|---|---|---|---|
| Self-esteem | Violence | 20.85 | 3.96 | 96 |
| | No violence | 20.69 | 2.82 | 16 |
| | Total | 20.83 | 3.81 | 112 |
| Social support | Violence | 34.64 | 5.53 | 96 |
| | No violence | 36.81 | 5.15 | 16 |
| | Total | 34.95 | 5.51 | 112 |
| Sense of belonging | Violence | 33.38 | 5.42 | 96 |
| | No violence | 34.06 | 4.79 | 16 |
| | Total | 33.47 | 5.32 | 112 |
| Social action | Violence | 2.08 | 1.65 | 96 |
| | No violence | 1.25 | 1.23 | 16 |
| | Total | 1.96 | 1.62 | 112 |

sis of variance for the differences between groups in terms of empowerment variables.

Empowerment practice shifts the focus from victim-blaming approaches that emphasize the perceived interpersonal deficiencies of women who experience violence and abuse to an examination of the strengths, resources, and capacity of women, as well as the structural dynamics within society that promote oppression based strategies of power and control. Empowerment practice targets three dimensions, including the personal, interpersonal, and political. These multidimensional and interwoven elements of empowerment provide the impetus for:

- Challenging personal attitudes and perceptions embedded in experiences of powerlessness;
- Strengthening knowledge and interpersonal skills to identify and pursue options;
- Improving one's ability to access services and resources; and
- Engaging in behaviors and actions to resist, overcome, and end oppression based violence and abuse on multiple levels.

Statistical tests used to determine whether significant differences existed between the group of women who had experienced violence and abuse compared with the group of women who had not experienced violence and abuse show no statistically significant differences on self-esteem, social support, and sense of belonging. Given the large proportion of the study participants who experienced violence and abuse, it is also recognized that meaningful differences when this condition occurs can be more difficult to detect. Based on existing literature, it was anticipated that women who had experienced violence and abuse would report lower scores on self-esteem, social support, sense of belonging, and social action.

## Self-Esteem

Low self-esteem has been one of the most commonly identified consequences of VAAW and outcomes most frequently targeted in the response to women who have experienced violence and abuse. The initial statistical tests reported women who had experienced violence and abuse had similar self-esteem scores as those who had not been abused.

In a 1999 study on urban American Indian identity, Walters[34] reported that, as education and income levels increased, self-esteem increased, thus promoting positive identity. The design for this study compared two independent samples from a population of college women, with no significant differences on self-esteem scores when looking at the groups as a whole. It is unknown whether self-esteem scores are higher for women who have experienced violence and abuse and are pursuing education compared with those who have experienced violence and abuse but do not have the opportunity to pursue education. This factor may account for the lack of statistically significant differences in this study. Regardless of the experience of violence and abuse, both groups of women in the 2004 study[35] were pursuing the promise of higher education and the choices that become available with such a decision.

When self-esteem was investigated by the age of experiencing violence and abuse, self-esteem scores significantly differed for women with adolescent or adult versus childhood experiences. Women who had not experienced violence and abuse as teens or adults had higher self-esteem scores than those who had experienced violence and abuse. Women who lived on reservations or tribal lands also reported higher self-esteem scores than those living in city/urban areas. Although these scores were not statistically significant, they are culturally significant. Self-esteem scores were lower when violence or abuse occurred in adolescence, in adulthood, or if the participant was raised in non-reservation settings. Experiencing violence as a child or participating in social/cultural activities did not affect self-esteem. In sum, the predicators of high self-esteem scores were:

- *Whether* a woman experienced violence and abuse;
- *When* a woman experienced violence and abuse (at what life stage: child, adolescent, or adult); and *Where* a woman was raised.

---

34. Walters (1999).
35. Chenault (2004).

These findings suggest that while the development of self-esteem is susceptible to violence and abuse, it may also be reinforced or strengthened by additional protective factors that exist in the community in which one is raised. Despite the challenges that exist in some reservation communities, the multiple regression analysis for this study suggests the dynamics unique to reservation cultures may serve as a protective factors that have a positive impact on self-esteem rather than diminishing one's belief in self, despite the adversity faced.

## Social Support and Sense of Belonging

Like self-esteem, both social support and a sense of belonging are often targeted in intervention practice and in the research on best practices in the field of violence and abuse. One dynamic of the cycle of violence and abuse is social isolation. This tactic effectively restricts, reduces, or eliminates ones contacts with sources of potential support and strains or severs connections to family, friends, and resources.

In terms of either social support or sense of belonging, no statistically significant findings were noted on comparison of the group of women who had experienced violence and abuse with the group of women who had not experienced violence and abuse. However, when additional tests analyzed where the participants had been raised, women who were raised on reservations, tribal lands, pueblos, or villages had statistically significant higher scores for both social support and sense of belonging than those who lived in urban areas or in rural non-reservation areas. Again, these findings suggest that reservations, tribal lands, pueblos, and villages foster environments and relationships that nurture social support networks and the sense of belonging, thus contributing to levels of empowerment for First Nations women by buffering women in these communities from the pathogenic effects of violence and abuse.

## Social Action

The third dimension of empowerment in this study—social action—is often the element for which the least amount of attention is focused, particularly in intervention research on violence against women, yet it is the most critical dimension of empowerment. This dimension emphasizes the importance of taking action and engaging in behaviors that seek to create change in systems, whether family, community, society, nation, or global systems. Because the intent of the study was to advance the knowledge base on culturally based empowerment practice or Indigenous empowerment, initial conceptualization of this variable explored what social action might look like from a tribal perspective. Walters,[36] in research on cultural affiliation, describes the connection to communities by involvement, advocacy, or participation in cultural traditions at the family, tribal, and government levels, as well as spiritual, political, or cultural participation at the community levels. Such activities and actions are instrumental in achieving a positive group identity, were consistent with an empowerment framework, and were subsequently used in the construction of a series of questions related to social action. These were transformed into a new variable, *social action*, which describes *participation in spiritual, political, or cultural activities in tribal communities that promote social action or change.*

Participants were queried about participation in cultural activities, such as traditional ceremonies or activities; participation in women's cultural activities, such as talking circles; or participation in cultural healing practices or ceremonies, such as sweat lodges. Most respondents (74%) reported participation in traditional cultural ceremonies, with a minority of participants (25.8%) reporting no participation. This finding indicates that, despite the history of oppression endured by First Nations People, these women maintain a high level of cultural connection or affiliation that potentially buffers them from external stressors, such as violence and abuse. While cultural connection in isolation may not be statistically significant, it becomes so when it is examined with social or political action. A moderate level of women (43%) reported involvement or participation in activities consistent with social action.

---

36. Walters (1999).

The second item explored participation in positive social change activities in tribal communities, such as education about VAAIW or engaging in activities seeking to change laws, policies, or programs for women who have experienced violence or abuse. Most participants (57%) reported no involvement in social action/change; however, 42.8% did participate in these activities. These variables were subsequently transformed into a new variable, *social action*, which describes *participation in spiritual, cultural, political or cultural activities in tribal communities that promote social action or change.* Women who had been threatened had higher scores on social action—again, an inverse relationship is found between being threatened and social action. Indigenous women who are threatened have higher rates of social action than those who have not been threatened.

There were also statistically significant differences on social action scores between groups (woman who experienced violence versus no violence) for women who had experienced emotional abuse. This finding suggests an inverse relationship exists between emotional abuse and social action. Tribal women who had experienced emotional abuse reported higher scores on social action compared with those who had not experienced emotional abuse. Findings from a multiple regression analysis indicated that social action is predicted by experiences of violence and abuse, specifically, emotional abuse and being threatened correlate with the use of a traditional healer or ceremonies. This finding suggests women in this sample who have experienced emotional abuse or been threatened are more likely to engage in social action, as well as the use of cultural practices (traditional healer or ceremonies) for preventing harm to oneself, protecting oneself, or correcting injustices to oneself.

## Other Responses to Violence and Abuse

Four items were included in the survey about the response of participants to experiences of violence and abuse. Most women do not report violence and abuse to the police or talk to professionals when violence and abuse happen—this response is magnified for women of color. As shown in **Table 5.11**, when asked whether the

Table 5.11  Report to Police ($N = 87$)

| Reporting Response | Frequency ($n$) | Percent (%) |
|---|---|---|
| No, incident not reported | 37 | 65.5 |
| Yes, incident reported | 30 | 34.5 |

Table 5.12  Cross-Tabulation for Type of
Violence and Police Report

| Type of Violence | Reported ($n/N$) | Percent (%) | Model Statistic |
|---|---|---|---|
| Being threatened | 18/29 | 62.0 | $x2$ (1, N = 87) = 14.65, $p = .000^*$ Cramer's V = .41 |
| Being stalked | 16/30 | 53.3 | $x2$ (1, N = 87) = 7.202, $p = .007^*$ Cramer's V = .28 |
| Sexual | 16/39 | 41.0 | $x2$ (1, N = 87) = 1.33, $p = .247$ Cramer's V = .12 |
| Physical | 28/69 | 40.5 | $x2$ (1, N = 87) = 5.48, $p = .019^*$ Cramer's V = .25 |
| Emotional | 28/77 | 36.3 | $x2$ (1, N = 86) = .709, $p = .400$ Cramers's V = .09 |

$^*$ p < .05

incident had been reported to the police, most participants (66%) had never reported the incident to the police, while 34% had reported the incident to the police. **Table 5.12** presents a cross-tabulation for the type of violence reported to police.

Similar findings were reported in relation to the use of helping professional. The use of helping professionals by women of color is often a "last resort" option, if used at all. As shown in **Table 5.13**, when asked whether a helping professional (social worker, psychologist, psychiatrist, counselor, or mental health professional) had been consulted about the incidents, 64% of the women reported they had never talked to a professional, while 36% reported they had talked to a professional. Instead, participants most often

### Table 5.13 Professional Consultation ($N = 96$)

| Professional Consultation* | Frequency ($n$) | Percent (%) |
|---|---|---|
| Never | 61 | 63.5 |
| Sometimes | 35 | 36.5 |

* Professional consultation is a consultation with a social worker, psychologist, psychiatrist, counselor, or mental health professional.

reported talking to a trusted friend or relative (53.1%), followed by always talking to a trusted friend or relative (32.2%), and then by never talking to a trusted friend or relative (13.5%), as shown in **Table 5.14**. This finding suggests community education approaches used by tribally based programs may strengthen systems of social support, more likely to be used by tribal women who experience violence and abuse. **Table 5.15** and **Table 5.16** present cross-tabulations for the type of violence discussed with a trusted friend or relative or a professional, respectively.

A series of correlation analyses showed six statistically significant correlations, with the strongest correlation between social support and a sense of belonging, indicating that as social support increases, a positive increase is also experienced in one's sense of belonging and self-esteem. The use of a traditional healer or ceremony was correlated with higher scores on social action and reporting the incident to the police, suggesting the use of traditional healing practices increases the likelihood of reporting the incident to the police, as well as engaging in social action. Talking to a professional was positively correlated with reporting the incident to the police, suggesting that Indigenous women who do obtain professional support are more likely to report violence and abuse to the police.

Reporting violence and abuse to the police was significantly more likely among those who had been threatened, those being stalked, and those who were physically victimized, although the strengths of these association using cross-tabulations was weak. Talking to a trusted friend or relative is significantly more likely for those who have been sexually victimized, although this relationship was also statistically weak. Talking to a professional is significantly more likely among those who have been threatened and those who have

Table 5.14  Talked to a Trusted Friend or Relative ($N = 95$)

| Talk with Trusted Friend or Relative | Frequency ($n$) | Percent (%) |
|---|---|---|
| Never talked | 13 | 13.7 |
| Sometimes talked | 51 | 53.7 |
| Always talked | 31 | 32.6 |

Table 5.15  Cross-Tabulation for Type of Violence and Talked to Trusted Friend or Relative

| Type of Violence | Talked with Friend/Relative ($n/N$) | Percent (%) | Model Statistic |
|---|---|---|---|
| Being threatened | 29/31 | 93.5 | $x2$ (1, N = 95) = 4.11, $p = .128$ Cramer's V = .20 |
| Being stalked | 27/30 | 90.0 | $x2$ (2, N = 95) = .655, $p = .72$ Cramer's V = .08 |
| Physical | 64/73 | 87.6 | $x2$ (2, N = 95) = 3.46, $p = .17$ Cramer's V = .19 |
| Sexual | 35/40 | 87.5 | $x2$ (2, N = 95) = 8.34, $p = .01^*$ Cramer's V = .29 |
| Emotional | 73/85 | 85.8 | $x2$ (2, N = 94) = .593, $p = .74$ Cramer's V = .07 |

been sexually victimized; however, the strength of these associations is weak.

The use of a traditional healer or ceremonies to overcome experiences of violence and abuse was significantly associated with those who had been stalked or been threatened, with the strongest relationship between the use of a traditional healer and being threatened. Table 5.17 presents data for the use of a traditional healer or ceremony. These findings are also culturally significant as they suggest different forms of violence may be perceived and approached differently. Table 5.18 presents a cross-tabulation for the type of violence and the use of a traditional healer.

### Table 5.16  Cross-Tabulation for Type of Violence and Talked to a Professional

| Type of Violence | Professional Consultation ($n/N$) | Percent (%) | Model Statistic |
|---|---|---|---|
| Being threatened | 16/31 | 51.6 | $x2$ (1, N = 96) = 4.53, $p$ = .03* Cramer's V = .21 |
| Sexual | 19/40 | 47.5 | $x2$ (1, N = 96) = 3.60, $p$ = .05* Cramer's V = .19 |
| Being stalked | 14/30 | 46.6 | $x2$ (1, N = 96) = 1.96, $p$ = .16 Cramer's V = .14 |
| Emotional | 34/85 | 40.0 | $x2$ (1, N = 95) = 3.46, $p$ = .06 Cramer's V = .19 |
| Physical | 29/74 | 39.1 | $x2$ (1, N = 96) = 1.03, $p$ = .30 Cramer's V = .10 |

### Table 5.17  Use of a Traditional Healer or Ceremony ($N = 94$)

| Use of Traditional Healer/Ceremony | Frequency ($n$) | Percent (%) |
|---|---|---|
| Never | 43 | 45.7 |
| Once | 28 | 29.8 |
| Twice | 12 | 12.8 |
| Three times or more | 11 | 11.7 |

### Table 5.18  Cross-Tabulation for Type of Violence and Use of a Traditional Healer/Ceremony

| Type of Violence | Use of Traditional Healer/Ceremony ($n/N$) | Percent (%) | Model Statistic |
|---|---|---|---|
| Being stalked | 19/30 | 63.3 | $x2$ (3, N = 94) = 8.18, $p$ = .04* Cramer's V = .29 |
| Physical | 39/73 | 53.4 | $x2$ (3, N = 94) = 5.40, $p$ = .14 Cramer's V = .24 |
| Emotional | 44/83 | 53.0 | $x2$ (3, N = 87) = .804, $p$ = .84 Cramer's V = .09 |
| Sexual | 20/40 | 50.0 | $x2$ (3, N = 94) = 3.93, $p$ = .26 Cramer's V = .20 |
| Being threatened | 15/31 | 48.3 | $x2$ (3, N = 94) = 11.71, $p$ = .008* Cramer's V = .35 |

# Chapter Six

# Research Method: Strengths and Limitations

*As my daughter learns to negotiate high school, the cliques and strongholds of privilege, I am reminded of the difficulty of being and raising [a] strong Indigenous [woman]. We face oppression on many levels and in virtually every structure and system, including relationships in which we are less valued as companions and wives. The added trauma of misogynist violence in our homes, family, communities and the larger society we interact with daily can produce a tremendous burden* (Chenault, 2010, personal communication).

The conditions faced by Indigenous women in contemporary society provide valuable insight into the current state of traditional tribal cultures, the strengths, philosophies, values, and belief that undergird First Nations civilizations. This value is as true today as it has been historically. So important are the roles and respect traditionally accorded Indigenous women that beliefs about women are central to the traditional philosophies of First Nations People and reflected in the teachings and ceremonies across tribal Nations in the United States and elsewhere.

Despite the beliefs and practices of tribes that promote attitudes of respect for women, Indigenous women are also confronted with multiple and disproportionate levels of violence and abuse that contradict the core philosophies common to many First Nations. At first glance, it would appear the historical burden of colonization and the ongoing oppression of Indigenous women by tactics such as violence and abuse had finally brought about the defeat of First

Nations Peoples. Despite the extraordinary levels of violence and abuse reported in this study, the findings suggest that, among the strong Indigenous women who participated in this study, their hearts are not on the ground, yet the problem cannot be ignored, hoping VAAIW will simply go away.

*Weaving Power, Weaving Strength* explores VAAIW using a theoretical framework grounded in decolonization and an Indigenous empowerment framework. While this work does not seek to continue the practice of *deficit thinking* or *victim-blaming* that has been so prevalent in much of the scholarship about tribal peoples, it is likely both the approach and findings will inevitably be deconstructed in this way. VAAIW is the contemporary manifestation of the multidimensional structural damage and disruption resulting from the Indigenous Holocaust in the Americas that threatens the survival of tribal Nations and should be approached with appropriate urgency.

The intent of this book is to offer a preliminary interdisciplinary approach to violence and abuse that uses critical analysis of this issue to understand VAAIW, as well as the long-term effects of violence and abuse on the traditional cultures of tribal Peoples and culturally based capacity-building. The book advances an exploratory model for Indigenous empowerment based upon analysis of structural disruption and the contemporary manifestation of colonization. *Weaving Power, Weaving Strength* seeks to replace deficit orientations of the past, by centering the strengths, teachings, cultural practices, and gendered teachings of Indigenous Nations.

There are multiple findings in this preliminary work that speak to the urgency for continued research on VAAIW and the importance of advocacy, practice, and social action change based on learning and living what culturally based Nations know; however, this work is not complete.

The research study provides further evidence of the spectrum of violence and abuse being experienced by Indigenous women and the prevalence and incidence of violence among tribal college women. It examines the relationship between violence and abuse, and the constructs associated with empowerment, specifically self-esteem, social support, sense of belonging, and social action. It provides insight into the responses of Indigenous women and the dynamics of this violence in tribal communities. The identification of limitations and potential for these findings, as well as the implications for ongoing research, are discussed further.

# Limitations of the Research Method

This study examined two primary research questions, the first being: *What is the lifetime prevalence and incidence of violence and abuse against Indigenous women (VAAIW) in a college sample of tribal women?* The second research question, on constructs associated with empowerment, asked: *Do significant differences exist between First Nations women who have experienced violence and abuse compared with those who have not experienced violence and abuse?*

While the findings related to prevalence and incidence in this study are consistent with recent studies on prevalence and incidence of violence,[1] the findings cannot be generalized or applied to all First Nations women or even all Indigenous college students because the sample was not randomly selected, nor is the sample representative of all Indigenous People, despite the tribal diversity represented. This study is important, however, in reporting both culturally significant findings and providing additional evidence of patterns of VAAIW that require further research to ensure tribal governments, programs, and organizations have baseline information to use when determining strategic planning priorities and making budgetary decisions. There are too many tribally based grant projects, with funding that is often dependent on data-based findings that are at risk for the loss of funding, simply because they lack research capacity to provide quantitative data that demonstrates the effectiveness of the strategies being used with Indigenous women. It is unacceptable to lose innovative tribal programs targeting VAAIW.

---

1. Bohn (2002); Buckwald, Tomita, Hartman, et al. (2000); Fairchild, Fairchild, & Stoner (1998); Hamby (2000); Harwell, Moore, & Spence (2003); Malcoe, Duran, & Montgomery (2004); Robin, Chester, & Rasmussen (1988).

The number of women who reported violence and abuse ($n =$ 96) in the study[2] compared with those who reported no violence and abuse ($n = 16$) suggests that young First Nations women remain at high risk for violence and abuse, despite the progress made by the Women's Movement, as well as by the Red Power Movement. The disproportionate number of women reporting violence compared with those who reported no violence limited the range of statistical tests appropriate for the analysis of the data and produced conditions that make it more difficult to detect meaningful differences between the two groups. While these statistical limitations must be acknowledged, the findings also speak to a phenomenon that has not been adequately examined and requires additional attention and funding.

There are limitations in terms of the extent to which the constructs used for the study reported (self-esteem, social support, sense of belonging, and social action) are the best or only indicators for determining empowerment. These variables were included in this study because they were consistent with empowerment and have been used in prior research on violence and abuse against women. This study advanced identified measurable outcomes for empowerment, but also sought to demonstrate the relationship between violence and abuse and levels of empowerment. There are no illusions about the usefulness of the exploratory study in solving VAAIW—instead, there is an opportunity to examine the many strands of work that should be addressed in larger discussions of violence and abuse and the impacts on the power of Indigenous women. Empowerment, like its antithesis, oppression, is equally multidimensional with interwoven layers of change required at multiple levels and, as such, generates unique measurement challenges, particularly when using quantitative approaches.

The measures used in the study, while consistent with those in other studies, require further evaluation for use with First Nations Peoples generally and Indigenous women specifically. For example, no statistically significant group differences were reported for self-esteem (violence group versus no violence group). However,

2. Chenault (2004).

statistically significant differences were identified in self-esteem scores for Indigenous women who had experienced violence and abuse as adolescents and adults, which suggest that self-esteem is affected by violence and abuse. An analysis of variance for differences between groups in terms of empowerment constructs is shown for childhood violence in **Table 6.1**, adolescent violence in **Table 6.2**, and adult violence in **Table 6.3**. Additionally, when participants were asked to self-identify the effects of violence and abuse, 80% reported lower self-esteem as a consequence of the experience of violence and abuse. **Table 6.4** presents the bivariate and partial correlations of the predictors for self-esteem. An analysis of variance for differences between groups in terms of empowerment constructs for the primary geographic location during childhood is presented in **Table 6.5**. These mixed findings are likely indicative of the differences in the way self-esteem is conceptualized among tribal women that existing scales do not adequately capture. The findings might also suggest tribal women are affected by violence and abuse in ways that differ from the constructs discussed in the literature and targeted in intervention practice in mainstream programs. Understanding self-esteem as defined in Indigenous populations and the role of self-esteem, if any, in the power of women, is one of the many important discussions needed with Indigenous women and tribal programs to ensure reliable research measures are developed and available for programs serving women, *if* it is determined that energy, time, and resources should be spent on constructs such as self-esteem.

Additional data are presented in the Tables regarding *t* tests for independent samples in terms of empowerment constructs. These Tables report constructs for the experiences of physical victimization (**Table 6.6**), emotional abuse (**Table 6.7**), being threatened (**Table 6.8**), being stalked (**Table 6.9**), and sexual victimization (**Table 6.10**).

The framework used for the analysis of violence and abuse recognizes the structural dynamics that perpetuate conditions of oppression; however, the design of this study fails to adequately evaluate the effects of structural violence on Indigenous women, arguably advancing deficit approaches to gender disruption, rather than structural models for change. Oppression-based VAAIW is cer-

Table 6.1 Analysis of Variance (ANOVA):
Differences between Groups by Childhood Violence and
Empowerment Constructs

| Empowerment Construct | Group | Mean | Standard Deviation | N |
|---|---|---|---|---|
| Self-esteem | Childhood violence | 20.49 | 4.41 | 39 |
| | No childhood violence | 21.11 | 3.64 | 57 |
| | Total | 20.85 | 3.96 | 96 |
| Social support | Childhood violence | 34.95 | 5.97 | 39 |
| | No childhood violence | 34.42 | 5.25 | 57 |
| | Total | 34.64 | 5.53 | 96 |
| Sense of belonging | Childhood violence | 33.54 | 4.89 | 39 |
| | No childhood violence | 33.26 | 5.79 | 57 |
| | Total | 33.38 | 5.42 | 96 |
| Social action | Childhood violence | 2.15 | 1.52 | 39 |
| | No childhood violence | 2.04 | 1.84 | 57 |
| | Total | 2.08 | 1.65 | 96 |

Table 6.2 Analysis of Variance (ANOVA):
Differences between Groups by Adolescent Violence and
Empowerment Constructs

| Empowerment Construct | Group | Mean | Standard Deviation | N |
|---|---|---|---|---|
| Self-esteem | Adolescent violence | 19.81 | 4.25 | 47 |
| | No adolescent violence | 21.86 | 3.42 | 49 |
| | Total | 20.85 | 3.96 | 96 |
| Social support | Adolescent violence | 33.94 | 5.68 | 47 |
| | No adolescent violence | 35.51 | 5.36 | 49 |
| | Total | 34.64 | 5.53 | 96 |
| Sense of belonging | Adolescent violence | 32.43 | 5.56 | 47 |
| | No adolescent violence | 34.29 | 5.18 | 49 |
| | Total | 33.38 | 5.42 | 96 |
| Social action | Adolescent violence | 2.00 | 1.57 | 47 |
| | No adolescent violence | 2.16 | 1.73 | 49 |
| | Total | 2.09 | 1.65 | 96 |

### Table 6.3  Analysis of Variance (ANOVA):
### Differences between Groups by Adult Violence and
### Empowerment Constructs

| Empowerment Construct | Group | Mean | Standard Deviation | N |
|---|---|---|---|---|
| Self-esteem | Adult violence | 20.25 | 2.86 | 71 |
| | No adult violence | 22.56 | 3.84 | 25 |
| | Total | 20.85 | 3.96 | 96 |
| Social support | Adult violence | 34.31 | 5.34 | 71 |
| | No adult violence | 35.56 | 6.04 | 25 |
| | Total | 34.64 | 5.53 | 96 |
| Sense of belonging | Adult violence | 33.03 | 5.51 | 71 |
| | No adult violence | 34.36 | 5.13 | 25 |
| | Total | 33.38 | 5.42 | 96 |
| Social action | Adult violence | 2.23 | 2.68 | 71 |
| | No adult violence | 1.68 | 1.52 | 25 |
| | Total | 2.08 | 1.65 | 96 |

### Table 6.4  Bivariate and Partial Correlations of the
### Predictors with Self-Esteem

| Predictors | Correlation between each predictor and self-esteem | Correlation between each predictor and self-esteem, controlling for all other predictors |
|---|---|---|
| Where primarily raised | .226** | .227 |
| Childhood violence and abuse | -.077 | -.112 |
| Adolescent violence and abuse | -.259*** | -.265 |
| Adult violence and abuse | -.256*** | -.337 |
| Social action | -.062 | -.110 |

$* p < .05$, $** p < .01$, $*** p < .001$

tainly characterized by behaviors such as physical and sexual violence against women, but it also be encountered daily in the hierarchical systems and practices of privilege, racism, and misogyny that undergird the larger society.

### Table 6.5 Analysis of Variance (ANOVA): Differences between Groups by "Where Primarily Raised" and Empowerment Constructs

| Empowerment Construct | Group | Mean | Standard Deviation | N |
|---|---|---|---|---|
| Self-esteem | City/urban | 20.15 | 4.24 | 55 |
| | Reservation, tribal land | 21.63 | 3.14 | 35 |
| | Rural—non-reservation | 20.85 | 3.34 | 20 |
| | Total | 20.83 | 3.81 | 112 |
| Social support | City/urban | 34.56 | 4.96 | 55 |
| | Reservation, tribal land | 36.31 | 5.49 | 34 |
| | Rural—non-reservation | 32.95 | 6.33 | 20 |
| | Total | 34.95 | 5.51 | 112 |
| Sense of belonging | City/urban | 32.65 | 5.33 | 55 |
| | Reservation, tribal land | 34.94 | 4.58 | 34 |
| | Rural—non-reservation | 32.55 | 6.03 | 20 |
| | Total | 33.47 | 5.32 | 112 |
| Cultural activities | City/urban | 1.11 | 1.03 | 55 |
| | Reservation, tribal land | 1.77 | 1.00 | 34 |
| | Rural—non-reservation | 1.00 | .795 | 20 |
| | Total | 1.31 | 1.02 | 112 |

* 2 non-responses in sample of 112.
   Note that the profile point, "Where primarily raised?" refers to the primary geographic location during childhood.

### Table 6.6 Independent Samples: *t* Test for Empowerment Constructs by Physical Victimization

| Variables | No Physical Victimization | Physical Victimization |
|---|---|---|
| Self-esteem | M = 21.26, SD = 3.108 | M = 20.61, SD = 4.134 |
| Social support | M = 35.03, SD = 6.193 | M = 34.91, SD = 5.174 |
| Sense of belonging | M = 33.42, SD = 5.53 | M = 33.50, SD = 5.248 |
| Social action | M = 1.61, SD = 1.32 | M = 2.15, SD = 1.733 |

Note: M, Mean; SD, standard deviation.

### Table 6.7  Independent Samples: *t* Test for Empowerment Constructs by Emotional Abuse

| Variables | No Emotional Abuse | Emotional Abuse |
|---|---|---|
| Self-esteem | M = 21.42, SD = 2.859 | M = 20.62, SD = 4.074 |
| Social support | M = 35.42, SD = 6.02 | M = 34.73, SD = 5.36 |
| Sense of belonging | M = 34.46, SD = 4.62 | M = 33.09, SD = 5.489 |
| Social action | M = 1.46, SD = 1.33 | M = 2.09, SD = 1.67* |

Note: M, Mean; SD, standard deviation.
Standard $t(109) = -1.76$, $p = .081$
Equal variances not assumed $t(51) = -1.987$, $*p = .052$

### Table 6.8  Independent Samples: *t* Test for Empowerment Constructs by Being Threatened

| Variables | Not Threatened | Threatened |
|---|---|---|
| Self-esteem | M = 21.51, SD = 3.50 | M = 20.00, SD = 4.487 |
| Social support | M = 35.10, SD = 5.28 | M = 34.55, SD = 6.136 |
| Sense of belonging | M = 33.81, SD = 5.18 | M = 32.58, SD = 5.667 |
| Social action | M = 1.75, SD = 1.445 | M = 2.52, SD = 1.93* |

Note: M, Mean; SD, standard deviation.
Standard $t(110) = -2.269$, $p = .025*$
Equal variances not assumed, $t(43) = -1.997$, $*p = .052$

### Table 6.9  Independent Samples: *t* Test for Empowerment Constructs by Being Stalked

| Variables | Not Stalked | Stalked |
|---|---|---|
| Self-esteem | M = 21.06, SD = 3.673 | M = 20.20, SD = 4.180 |
| Social support | M = 35.45, SD = 5.396 | M = 33.57, SD = 5.685 |
| Sense of belonging | M = 33.99, SD = 5.146 | M = 32.07, SD = 5.63 |
| Social action | M = 1.99, SD = 1.63 | M = 1.90, SD = 1.63 |

### Table 6.10  Independent Samples: *t* Test for Empowerment Constructs by Sexual Victimization

| Variables | No Sexual Victimization | Sexual Victimization |
|---|---|---|
| Self-esteem | M = 21.26, SD = 3.49 | M = 20.05, SD = 4.27 |
| Social support | M = 35.60, SD = 5.16 | M = 33.78, SD = 5.98 |
| Sense of belonging | M = 33.65, SD = 5.28 | M = 33.15, SD = 5.45 |
| Social action | M = 1.92, SD = 1.44 | M = 2.05, SD = 1.92 |

Despite these limitations, these findings are useful in advancing understanding of the scope of violence and abuse being experienced by First Nations women and underscore both the urgency and need for additional funding, research, and practice that build on the strengths of Indigenous Peoples, which recognize the structural dynamics that perpetuate such conditions. When this author initially began exploring gender and Indigenous women in the 1990s, the late Hunkpapa Lakota scholar, Bea Medicine, provided a reminder to focus on a piece of this work rather than feeling compelled to have all the answers. In this way, *Weaving Power, Weaving Strength* represents a beginning rather than a conclusion.

## Strength of the Research Method

There are limitations to this study as already discussed; however, there is also tremendous need and potential for future research, scholarship, and practice on the topic of VAAIW, especially approaches based on Indigenous research methodology, empowerment, and social justice. The study described is the first and only dissertation study in the United States that examines First Nations women and violence and abuse. It is the only study that explores the spectrum of VAAIW who are enrolled members of federally recognized tribes. It is the only study that examines violence and abuse across the lifetime and the only study that examines the relationship between violence and abuse on constructs associated with empowerment. Although more recent health-care studies have focused on intimate partner violence in tribal health clinics, there are no studies exploring the effects of violence and abuse on the power of women, as measured by self-esteem, sense of belonging, social support, and social action of Indigenous women or any other studies examining the effect of violence on Indigenous women's power, as defined by Indigenous women.

The 2004 study reported in this book on VAAIW is unique in its examination of the range of violence experienced across a tribally diverse population (39 tribes were represented) of relatively young Indigenous women from throughout the United States. Items contained in the survey advance the importance of examining the relationship between culture, empowerment, women, and violence for future research. This study has contributed to the knowledge base within the disciplines of Social Work and Indigenous Studies about violence and abuse, using participatory action methods. It provides a practical example of processes that might be considered as a framework for future research on culturally based empowerment practice and research with communities of color. Certainly, future scholars will find there is much to be learned from the approaches used in this book, both strengths and challenges, as Indigenous research methodology is advanced.

Rather than imposing a researcher-driven model for this study, the study utilized elements of empowerment-based and participatory action research, although these elements should be expanded further. Approaches emphasizing collaboration with underserved communities on issues of concern with the intent of developing critical consciousness and social action to transform systems and relationships within and between these systems will likely produce better surveys, constructs, methods, and findings. There are weaknesses in these approaches in this study. Conversations about VAAIW in formal and informal settings generated many opportunities to reflect upon the incongruence between violence and abuse and what Indigenous Peoples are taught culturally. Initially, conversations about violence against Indigenous women occurred in settings with tribal students, family, friends, and colleagues working in the field. As innovative programs were identified from these initial conversations, contacts were made with tribal women who followed traditional practices, as well as women working in the field. These discussions contributed to the conceptualization of the study, which was then presented to larger groups of women and tribal communities through presentations on the topic in workshop and conference settings attending by Indigenous Peoples and tribal governments, creating a "snowball effect." The consciousness generated by talking honestly about the truth of VAAIW and reflecting upon the social and cultural significance of this phenomenon has raised interest and awareness and will continue to prompt social action and social change at multiple levels. Lessons learned from the prior study, ongoing reflection about the benefit of quantitative versus qualitative research and the fit of the approach used with more recent work on Indigenous research methodology are being woven together for use with tribal governments who have prioritized research on the topic of VAAIW using tribal resources.

This work does not pretend to be a definitive examination of VAAIW or even a full accounting of the best tribal practices or strategies for ending this phenomenon. Instead, it shares a promising theoretical framework for understanding violence and abuse that seeks to build on the strengths and resources within tribal communities and that acknowledges the role of colonialism in contributing to the contemporary problem and patterns of violence and abuse. It introduces students in Social Work, Indigenous Studies, and Women's Studies to the problem of violence against Indigenous women and encourages analysis of the structural and cultural dynamics that have undermined the role, status, and contributions of tribal women. Ideally, it raises the consciousness of those outside tribal communities of the invaluable contributions of grassroots activists, scholars, and crises intervention, health care, and resource providers who have been addressing this issue, as well as the exceptional programs that exist throughout the United States and renegade scholarship, invisible in much of the mainstream scholarship and literature.

While this study addresses VAAIW, the nature of the framework may also lend itself to use with other issues and other communities of color. It does not advocate deficit approaches, but calls upon a new generation of activists, scholars, and professional helpers, especially social workers, to engage in practice that advances cultural competence, social justice, and social action by confronting the structural dynamics that perpetuate systems of domination, oppression, and subordination that are alive and well.

Practice approaches that address the structural dynamics of oppression, power, and control are central to ending violence and abuse against women, yet are virtually non-existent in much of the mainstream literature. The lack of attention to these issues ensures a primary focus susceptible to blaming women, instead of on the structural conditions that promote violence against women. There are specific changes needed to integrate such understandings into future work, which include but are not limited to:

- Indigenous empowerment as a catalyst for social change;
- Practice sensitive to grief associated with the trauma of violence and abuse and oppression;
- Valuing culturally based empowerment practice;
- Valuing empowerment-based research methodologies;
- Strengthening curriculum on violence and abuse;
- Evaluating issues of disparity in court systems, sentencing, and honoring alternative forms of justice and healing; and
- Expanding funding to include innovative research-based practice initiatives.

## Indigenous Empowerment as a Catalyst for Social Change

The findings from this study magnify the importance of challenging personal and professional assumptions about women who experience violence and abuse and how practice, intervention, and research on the issues of violence and abuse should be designed. Despite the astounding level of violence and abuse reported, the findings of this study suggest that other factors also mitigate the sense of powerlessness associated with violence and abuse that motivate women to persevere despite the circumstance experienced. Table 6.11 presents the correlations among empowerment and responses to violence and abuse.

Engaging women who experience violence and abuse in social action to challenge oppression becomes a tool for building on inherent strengths and has the power to serve as an antitoxin to themes of powerlessness, shame, and helplessness confronted by women. In doing so, women who own and acknowledge their power serve as an impetus for powerful social change. Innovative practice that integrates existing knowledge and cultural wisdom while incorporating analysis of the structural dynamics of oppression within practice and policy may provide a necessary shift to trigger long-term change toward ending VAAIW. Women who have been *dis-*

## Table 6.11 Correlations between Empowerment and Responses to Violence and Abuse

| Response | Report | Talk | Consult | Heal | Support | Belong | Action | Esteem |
|---|---|---|---|---|---|---|---|---|
| Police report | -.130 | | | | | | | |
| Talk with friend/relative | .319* | .046 | | | | | | |
| Professional consult | .314* | .156 | .029 | | | | | |
| Use of healer/ceremony | .131 | .189 | .027 | .238 | | | | |
| Social support | -.085 | .120 | -.065 | .051 | .750* | | | |
| Sense of belonging | .133 | .042 | .146 | .452* | .168 | .052 | | |
| Social action | -.001 | .079 | -.076 | -.057 | .324* | .337* | -.011 | |
| Self-esteem | | | | | | | | |

* Correlation significant at the .005 level (2-tailed).

empowered by the oppression of violence and abuse are not "just victims" but instead are activists, allies, and key stakeholders whose passion to survive and wisdom in overcoming adversity is needed to enhance understanding of what constitutes best practice in disciplines such as social work. While the movement to challenge gender-based oppression is currently 40 years old, significant challenges remain in the structures that shape societal attitudes about violence and abuse against women, as well as the development and implementation of policy cognizant of the forces that must be dealt with to end violence and abuse against women. Practice that supports women in repatriating and reconnecting to knowledge, power, and wisdom, subjugated by the systems, values, and practices of oppression, ensures the continued survival of a counterforce of resistance to misogynistic practices and policies.

## Practice Sensitive to Grief Associated with the Trauma of Violence and Abuse and Oppression

The physical, intellectual, emotional, and spiritual trauma experienced by women oppressed by violence and abuse is similar to that experienced by other oppressed groups, in that both phenomenon have been associated with interpersonal feelings of powerlessness, helplessness, shame, guilt, and self-blame. Practice and policy approaches that compound the sense of powerlessness by focusing on individual shortcomings magnify the sense of shame and guilt common to those who find themselves in situations beyond their control. The dynamics of grief associated with multiple traumas and ongoing losses accompanying oppression and VAAIW must be recognized an integral to long-term processes of reclaiming power.

The willingness to critique the multiple levels of interpersonal and structural dynamics that support violence against women is particularly appropriate for consideration for women as a group who are oppressed both by colonization and violence and abuse. Examinations of the reality of oppression experienced by First Nations People should not be viewed as an effort to blame institutions or the environment for present conditions. Instead, this work

should be considered as a necessary step toward healing and rec-
onciliation that promotes talking honestly about the truth. The existing wisdom, strength, and power of women, families, and
communities who have experienced systematic and institutionalized
oppression and discrimination must be validated and used in practice and policy rather than ignored and denied because it is too uncomfortable.

Such approaches are characteristic of tribal practitioners and
programs responding to VAAIW. The emphasis on engaging entire
communities in healing from the trauma of history and raising
consciousness of the extent to which this history has warped tribal
values, beliefs, and practice has inspired social action and social
change in many tribal communities on Indigenous terms. The re-
alization that comes with talking honestly about the truth enables
many to disengage from cultural shame and self-hate to pursue behaviors and practices grounded in cultural wisdom.

# Valuing Culturally-Based Empowerment Practice

The colonization of Indigenous Peoples has contributed to the
adoption of individual, family, and community behaviors in some
tribal settings that tolerate and normalize the oppression of women,
as well as VAAIW, yet analysis of gender has been inadequate in
much of the literature on Indigenous colonization. This absence
of literature has rendered invisible the misogynistic nature of colonization and obscured the contemporary manifestations of such
practices.

Consideration of the cultural and value contexts operating in
communities is important when structural change of such conditions is desired. Increasingly, a new generation of Indigenous feminists is advancing critical inquiry in these areas. The use of cultural
values, beliefs, and practices can be important tools to empowerment at multiple levels. Tribal responses to VAAIW may emerge
from a spiritual-cultural belief versus a social work or academic
theoretical perspective, and these beliefs should be respected. Among
many tribal peoples, acts of violence against women may be viewed

as evidence of cultural disharmony that must be corrected through ceremonies versus the courts. Empowerment-based activities to raise consciousness counter hegemonic practice and policy by approaching violence using alternative theoretical and cultural perspectives. Tribal programs responding to violence are often at the epicenter of work examining the consequences of structural disruption and colonization.

## Valuing Empowerment-Based Research Methodologies

Empowerment frameworks are not intended to be exclusively applied to practice but also extend to the methodologies used in research and social policy development. The 2004 research study[3] integrated a theoretical framework of empowerment in the research process, as well as in the overall design of the study. Using participatory action research methods, information about the study has been shared with stakeholders and feedback has been integrated throughout the research design process. Processes that promoted dialogue with stakeholders were used to check the appropriateness of the overall approach and areas of weakness in existing responses as well as to explore the integration and usefulness of existing outcomes for tribally based programs for which funding is increasingly tied to such outcomes. Intentional efforts were made to design a quantitative study that was culturally sensitive, that identified the strengths of First Nations communities while preventing harm and maximizing benefits to tribal communities, yet these efforts could be strengthened greatly.

## Strengthening Curriculum on Violence and Abuse

Increasingly, practice in this field is no longer an issue of responding to or preventing domestic violence but one of education

---

3. Chenault (2004).

about, prevention of, and response to a wide range of gender and race-based violence targeted at First Nations women and others. Curriculum that prepares practitioners and organizers to respond to diverse forms and multiple dynamics of violence and oppression must be considered. Sensitivity to the cultural dynamics mediated by geography and the development of culturally specific practice skills that are responsive to the needs of both urban and reservation Indigenous women is paramount.

Clearly, the findings of this study suggest tribal women in urban settings are at risk and often without services responsive to the dynamics of culture. Programs, services, curriculum, intervention, and practices that fail to meaningful integrate content regarding the needs and issues of marginalized and urban tribal communities are counterproductive, and the need is urgent to respond more effectively to Indigenous women in these circumstances.

*Social Policy Implications.* It is critical to address policy oversight within VAWA[4] that erodes the rights of self-determination and sovereignty as the Act relates to jurisdictional issues and conflicts, recognition of court orders, and prevailing cultural and traditional components of justice within Indigenous Nations.[5] The continued failure to address adequate funding for urban programs that respond to violence against Indigenous women must be corrected. The unique political status of First Nations People and the specific legal rights of self-governance must be honored in policy formulations and legislation. It is a mockery of tribal self-determination to include funding provisions that subvert existing tribal social systems by requiring submission to failed Western notions of punishment and pathology in order to qualify for needed services. Language is needed that recognizes and honors traditional Indigenous systems of restorative justice and ensures equitable dis-

---

4. Violence Against Women Act (VAWA) (1994); Violence Against Women Act (VAWA) — Victims of Trafficking and Violence Protection Act (2000); Violence Against Women and Department of Justice Reauthorization Act (2005).

5. Luna, Ferguson, Williams, Jr., et al. (2002).

tribution of funding to address the multidimensional nature of violence.

Current approaches to funding STOP Violence Against Indian Women[6] have been limited to reservation programs because of language within the legislation limiting eligibility to recognized tribal governments. Tribes have a government-to-government relationship with the federal government based on the unique political status and the trust responsibility of the federal government. As quasi-sovereign entities, tribes have successfully negotiated provisions and a share of resources within the VAWA[7] responsive to the needs of tribal people living on reservations or tribal lands. Such negotiations must be extended to include Indigenous women off-reservation as well as an estimated two-thirds of all tribal women who live in urban areas and are ineligible for STOP funds. As the findings of the 2004 study reported,[8] two-thirds of the violence and abuse experienced occurred in urban areas or cities.

This point is not to suggest these funds should be shifted from programs providing services to reservations, tribal lands, pueblos, and villages but instead *new* earmarked funds for urban tribal programs are needed. Without attention to the prevalence and incidence of violence and abuse experienced by urban tribal women, a much-needed safety net is non-existent. By amending eligibility requirements to include the language, "*Indigenous victim assistance programs providing services to urban or reservation based First Nations women,*" the needs of tribal women can be responded to more effectively. Funding levels for existing programs should be legislatively protected to ensure funds for urban women do not come at the expense of reservation-based programs and services. As the findings in this study report, reservations remain the repository of Indigenous cultural wisdom and the resources for building cultural

---

6. United States Department of Justice, Office of Violence Against Women. (n.d.).

7. Violence Against Women Act (VAWA) (1994); VAWA—Victims of Trafficking and Violence Protection Act (2000); Violence Against Women and Department of Justice Reauthorization Act (2005).

8. Chenault (2004).

capacity in infrastructures devastated by policies of colonialism and should not be devalued by funding decisions that pit reservation programs against urban programs.

## Evaluating Issues of Disparity in Court Systems, Sentencing, and Honoring Alternative Forms of Justice and Healing

Additional analysis of existing disparity in justice for Indigenous men is needed. Clearly, tribal men who engage in VAAIW must be held accountable for their actions; however, First Nations men should not be held to more severe standards or multiple prosecutions for such acts. Greater flexibility is needed in existing policy to ensure alternative forms of justice and healing are recognized in tribal communities. A study of the Navajo peacemaking system reported this approach to be an effective tool in solving family conflict.[9] In this study, 29% of peacemaking participants experienced a reoccurrence of the problem versus 64% who used the family court system. Despite the promise of restorative-justice approaches, the dynamics of violence and community must be further evaluated to avoid re-victimization of women in these tribal systems and communities, as anecdotally reported in conversations with tribal women. In some cases, it would be far less expensive culturally and economically to support traditional systems of justice rather than imposing bureaucratic replicas of the mainstream justice system. Movement toward traditional systems of justice will not be any more successful than mainstream justice systems if ongoing attention to the extent to which oppressive ideologies, beliefs, and practices inherent to oppression are not continually challenged. Raising consciousness of the extent to which traditional systems have been contaminated over history by philosophies of domination is essential if nation-building that seeks to restore culturally viable social structures in tribal communities is to occur, including justice and peacemaking systems.

---

9. Gross (2001).

## Expanding Funding to Include Innovative Research-Based Practice Initiatives

Currently, VAIW programs may fund direct services that include crises intervention, emergency shelters, crises hotlines, mental health counseling, victim advocacy, emergency transportation of victims, court advocacy, and the provision of bilingual services. Support for Indigenous researchers is notably lacking. Research using Indigenous methodologies and frameworks, such as empowerment, are needed to further evaluate the effectiveness of existing practice in the field, particularly with women of color. Finally, additional support is needed for First Nations graduate research fellowships in order to attract and prepare the next generation of tribal scholars and researchers.

# Conclusion

The use of empowerment frameworks with communities of culture is particularly relevant as discussions of best practice with disenfranchised populations are considered. However, the dilemmas are numerous for practitioners and researchers on the topic of violence and abuse with Indigenous Nations. Existing outcomes typically used in mainstream research, may be inconsistent with the theoretical orientation of empowerment and may conflict with the way these terms are valued and used within tribal Nations. The power of tribal women who remain connected to the traditional cultures of Indigenous Nations is more likely situated in the indigenousness of this experience and derived from action-oriented commitment to advancing the sovereignty and survival of First Nations, despite the adversity of experiences of violence and abuse. While the power of tribal women may be interrupted by experiences of violence and abuse, the protective factors of social support and belonging may mitigate these experiences and contribute to the resiliency of Indigenous women. Effective empowerment practice has not been well documented and is only recently being applied to the many fields of practice in social work and violence against women.

The literature is scant — and, for some, uncomfortable to consider — that examines the intersections between colonization and oppression, violence and women, the power of tribal women as defined by tribal women, and the experiences of Indigenous women and best practices for reconnecting women who have been disconnected from their power. The role of social workers as historical participants in the oppression of Indigenous Peoples and the consequent distrust of the profession in many tribal communities cannot be ignored. These issues require careful consideration as issues such as violence and abuse are addressed.

Approaches that incorporate analysis of the structural factors that have contributed to the oppression of cultural institutions and systems in subjugating marginalized populations constitute innovation in the approaches used. Flexible strategies promoting the integration and utilization of existing strengths, capacity, and resources; consciousness-raising activities and social action; and policy development and legislation are needed. The challenge for professionals, academics, social work practitioners, and researchers alike will be found in their ability to work collaboratively with grassroots scholars, practitioners, and activists in communities who are conscious of the strengths and capacity that exist despite the challenges faced. Until that time, intermediary roles will be assumed as empowerment is operationalized in ways that fulfill federal requirements and that communities are supported in the development and strengthening of culturally grounded innovative practice. Without examination of the structural forces that have triggered inequalities and oppression, victim-blaming, stereotypes, and failed social policy and practice will continue to hinder effective intervention and lasting social change.

# References

Adam, B. D. (1978). *The survival of domination: Inferiorization in everyday life.* New York: Elsevier.

Albers, P., & Medicine, B. (1983). *The hidden half: Studies of Plains Indian women.* Lanham, MD: University Press of America.

Albert, M., Cagan, L., Chomsky, N., Hahnel, R., King, M., Sargent, L., & Sklar, H. (1986). *Liberating theory.* Cambridge, MA: South End Press.

Alfred, T. (1999). *Peace, power, righteousness: An indigenous manifesto.* Don Mills, ON: Oxford University Press.

Almeida, R. (1993). Unexamined assumptions and service delivery systems: Feminist theory and racial exclusions. *Journal of Feminist Family Therapy, 5,* 3–23.

Amnesty International (2007). United States of America: Maze of injustice: The failure to protect indigenous women from violence. *Amnesty International Report AMR 51/035/2007.* Retrieved March 24, 2010, from http://www.amnesty.org/en/library/info/AMR51/035/2007.

Amnesty International. (2009). Canada: No more stolen sisters: A human rights response to discrimination and violence against indigenous women in Canada. *Amnesty International Report AMR 20/012/2009.* Retrieved February 13, 2009, from http://www.amnesty.ca/stolensisters/amr2000304.pdf.

Anderson, K. (1985). Commodity exchange and subordination: Montagnais-Naskapi and Huron women, 1600–1650. *Journal of Women in Culture and Society, 11*(1), 48–62.

Bachman, R. (1992). *Death and violence on the reservation: Homicide, family violence, and suicide in American Indian populations.* Westport, CT: Auburn House.

Bandura, A. (1982). Self-efficacy mechanism in human agency. *American Psychologist, 37*(2), 122–147.

Bartky, S. L. (1990). *Femininity and domination: Studies in the phenomenology of oppression (thinking gender).* New York: Routledge.

Bataille, G. M., & Sands, K. M. (1984). *American Indian women: Telling their lives.* Lincoln, NE: University of Nebraska Press.

Berk, R. A., Newton, P. J., & Berk, S. F. (1986). What a difference a day makes: An empirical study of the impact of shelters for battered women. *Journal of Marriage and the Family, 48*(August 1986), 481–490.

Blauner, R. (1969). Internal colonialism and ghetto revolt. *Social Problems, 16*(4), 393–408.

Bohn, D. K. (2002). Lifetime and current abuse, pregnancy risks, and outcomes among Native American women. *Journal of Health Care for the Poor and Underserved, 13*(2), 184–198.

Boyer, P., & Boyer, E. L. (1997). *Native American colleges: Progress and prospects: Special report (Carnegie Foundation for the Advancement of Teaching).* San Francisco, CA: Jossey-Bass, Inc.

Brave Heart, M. Y. H. (1998). The return to the sacred path: Healing the historical trauma and historical unresolved grief response among the Lakota through a psychoeducational group intervention. *Smith College Studies in Social Work, 68*(3), 287–305.

Brave Heart, M. Y. H., & DeBruyn, L. (1998). The American Indian holocaust: Healing historical unresolved grief. *American Indian and Alaska Native Mental Health Research,* 60–82.

Buckwald, D., Tomita, S., Hartman, S., Furman, R., Dudden, M., & Manson, S., M. (2000). Physical abuse of urban Native Americans. *Journal of General Internal Medicine, 15*(8), 562–564.

Busch, N. B., & Valentine, D. (2000). Empowerment practice: A focus on battered women. *Affilia, 15*(1), 82–95.

Cangleska, Inc. (2000). *Violence against Oglala women is not Lakota tradition. South Dakota Coalition Against Domestic Violence and Sexual Assault.* Pierre, SD: Administration for Children and Families, Office of Community Services, U. S. Department of Health and Human Services.

Carlson, B. (1977). Battered women and their assailants. *Social Work, 22*, 455–460.

Carpio, M. V. (2004). American Indian women and sterilization abuse. *Social Justice, 31*(4), 40–53.

Chafetz, J. S. (Ed.). (1999). *Handbook of the sociology of gender.* New York: Kluwer Academic / Plenum Publishers.

Chapin, D. (1994). Peace on earth begins in the home. *The Circle, 14*(1).

Chenault, V. S. (2004). *Violence and abuse against indigenous women.* Unpublished doctoral dissertation. University of Kansas, School of Social Welfare, Lawrence.

Child, B. J. (1998). *Boarding school seasons: American Indian families, 1900–1940.* Lincoln, NE: University of Nebraska Press.

Classic Gaming. (2008). *Atari 2600 — Game of the Week: Custer's Revenge.* Retrieved March 24, 2010, from http://classicgaming. gamespy.com/View.php?view=GameMuseum.Detail&id=282.

Clear Channel Communications, Inc. (2010). *100.5 The Fox: Classic rock.* Retrieved March 24, 2010, from http://www.1005the fox.com/main.html.

Cohen, S., & Hoberman, H. M. (1983). Positive events and social supports as buffers of life change stress. *Journal of Applied Social Psychology, 13*, 99–125.

Collins, B. G. (1986). Defining feminist social work. *Social Work, 31* (May–June), 214–220.

Cook-Lynn, E. (2007). *New Indians, old wars.* Champaign, IL: University of Illinois Press.

Cox, E. O. (1991). The critical role of social action in empowerment oriented groups. *Social Work With Groups, 14*, 77–90.

Cox, J., & Stoltenberg, C. (1991). Evaluation of a treatment program for battered wives. *Journal of Family Violence, 6*(4), 395–413.

Crenshaw, K. (1991). Demarginalizing the intersection of race and sex: A Black feminist critique of antidiscrimination doctrine, feminist theory, and antiracist politics. In K. Bartlett & R. Kennedy (Eds.), *Feminist legal theory* (pp. 57–80). Boulder, CO: Westview.

Davis, L. V., Hagen, J. L., & Early, T. J. (1994). Social services for battered women: Are they adequate, accessible, and appropriate? *Social Work, 39*(6), 695–704.

Denetdale, J. N. (2009). Securing Navajo national boundaries: War, patriotism, tradition, and the Diné Marriage Act of 2005. *Wicazo Sa Review, 24*(2), 131–148.

Devens, C. (1992). *Countering colonization: Native women and Great Lakes missions, 1630–1900*. Berkeley, CA: University of California Press.

Dobyns, H. F. (1984). Native American population collapse and recovery. In W. R. Swagerty (Ed.), (pp. 17–35), *Scholars and the Indian experience: Critical reviews of recent writing in the social sciences*. Indiana University Press: Bloomington, IN.

Duran. E., & Duran, B. (1995). *Native American postcolonial psychology*. Albany, NY: State University of New York (SUNY) Press.

Enloe, C. (2000). *Maneuvers: The international politics of militarizing women's lives*. Berkeley, CA: University of California Press.

Fairchild, D. G., Fairchild, M. W., & Stoner, S. (1998). Prevalence of adult domestic violence among women seeking routine care in a Native American health care facility. *American Journal of Public Health 88*(10), 1515–1517.

Fire Thunder, C. (2000). *Violence against Indian women*. Presentation at Haskell Indian Nations University, Lawrence, KS.

Fleming, J. (1979). *Stopping wife abuse*. Garden City, NY: Anchor Press/Doubleday.

Foro Internacional de Mujeres Indigenas (FIMI) [International Indigenous Women's Forum] (2006). *Mairin Iwanka Raya: Indigenous women stand against violence—A companion report to the United Nations Secretary-General's study on violence against women*. Retrieved June 1, 2010, from http://www.un.org/esa/socdev/unpfii/documents/vaiwreport06.pdf.

Fowlkes, D. L. (1997). Moving from feminist identity politics to coalition politics through a feminist materialist standpoint of subjectivity in Gloria Anzaldúa's Borderlands/La Frontera: The New Mestiza. *Hypatia 12*(2), 105–124.

Freeman. E. M. (2001). *Substance abuse intervention, prevention, rehabilitation, and systems change strategies: Helping individuals, families, and groups to empower themselves.* New York: Columbia University Press.

Freire, P. (1970). *Pedagogy of the oppressed.* New York, Seabury Press.

Freire, P. (1998). *Education for critical consciousness.* New York: Continuum International Publishing Group.

Gil, D. G. (1998). *Confronting injustice and oppression: Concepts and strategies for social workers.* New York: Columbia University Press.

GlenMaye, L. (1998). Empowerment of women. In L. M. Gutierrez, R. J. Parsons, & E. O. Cox (Eds.), *Empowerment in social work practice: A sourcebook* (pp. 29–51). Pacific Grove, CA: Brooks/Cole Publishing Co.

Glesne, C., & Peshkin, A. (1992). *Becoming qualitative researchers: An introduction.* New York: Longman.

Green, L. L. (n.d.). *Sexual violence against Tutsi women in Rwanda in 1994.* Retrieved July 6, 2009, from http://www.author-me.com/nonfiction/sexualviolence.html.

Green, R. D. (1975). The Pocahontas perplex: The image of Indian women in American culture. *Massachusetts Review, 16*(4), 698–714.

Gross, E. K. (2001). *Evaluation/assessment of Navajo peacemaking.* Rockville, MD: National Criminal Justice Reference Service (NCJRS). Retrieved February 13, 2009, from http://www.ncjrs.gov/pdffiles1/nij/grants/187675.pdf.

Gunn Allen, P. (1992). *The sacred hoop: Recovering the feminine in American Indian traditions.* Boston: Beacon Press Books.

Gutierrez, L. M. (1991). *When Jesus came, the Corn Mothers went away: Marriage, sexuality, and power in New Mexico, 1500–1846.* Stanford, CA: Stanford University Press.

Gutierrez, L. M., & Ortega, R. (1991). Developing models to empower Latinos: The importance of groups. *Social Work with Groups, 14*(2), 23–43.

Gutierrez, L. M., Parsons, R. J., & Cox, E. O. (Eds.). (1998). *Empowerment in social work practice: A sourcebook.* Pacific Grove, CA: Brooks/Cole Publishing Co.

Hamby, S. L. (2000). The importance of community in a feminist analysis of domestic violence among American Indians. *American Journal of Community Psychology, 28*(5), 649–669.

Hartick, L. (1982). *Identification of personality characteristics and self-concept factors of battered wives.* Palo Alto, CA: R&E Research Associates, Inc.

Harwell, T. S., Moore, K. R., & Spence, M. R. (2003). Physical violence, intimate partner violence, and emotional abuse among adult American Indian men and women in Montana. *Preventive Medicine, 37*(4), 297–303.

Hodges, V., Burwell, Y., & Ortega, D. (1998). Empowering families. In L. M. Gutierrez, R. J. Parsons, & E. O. Cox (Eds.), *Empowerment in social work practice: A sourcebook* (pp. 146–162). Pacific Grove, CA: Brooks/Cole Publishing Co.

Hooks, B. (1995). *Killing rage: Ending racism.* New York: Henry Holt & Company.

Hurtado, A. (1997). Relating to privilege and political mobilization: Toward a multicultural feminism. In A. Hurtado (Ed.), *The color of privilege: Three blasphemies on race and feminism* (pp. 1–44). Ann Arbor, MI: University of Michigan Press.

INCITE, and Mantilla, K. (2002). *Color of violence 2002: Building a movement.* Retrieved June 13, 2010, from http://www.incite-national.org/index.php?s=62.

Jacobs, S. E. (1995). Continuity and change in gender roles at San Juan Pueblo. In L. F. Klein & L. A. Ackerman (Eds.), *Women and power in Native North America* (pp. 177–213). Norman, OK: University of Oklahoma Press.

Jaimes, M. A., & Halsey, T. (1992). *American Indian women: At the center of indigenous resistance in contemporary North America* (pp. 311–344). In M. A. Jaimes (Ed.). *The state of Native America: Genocide,· colonization and resistance.* Cambridge, MA: South End Press.

Jenkins, K. (1988). Working paper on Maori women and social policy. *Report of the Royal Commission of Social Policy, vol. III.* Wellington, New Zealand: Royal Commission of Social Policy.

Jones, J. (1981). *Bad blood: The Tuskegee syphilis experiment: A tragedy of race and medicine.* New York: Free Press.

Kitka, J. (2008). Someone explain the humor in brutalizing Native women. COMPASS: Points of view from the community. *Anchorage Daily News,* April 19, 2008. Retrieved March 24, 2010, from http://www.adn.com/2008/04/19/380596/someone-ex-plain-the-humor-in-brutalizing.html.

Klein, L. F., & Ackerman, L. A. (1995). *Women and power in native North America*. Norman, OK: University of Oklahoma Press.

LaFromboise, T. D., Berman, J.S., & Sohi, B. K. (1994). American Indian women. In L. Comas-Diaz & B. Greene (Eds.), *Women of color: Integrating ethnic and gender identities in psychotherapy* (pp. 30–71). New York: Guilford Press.

LaFromboise, T. D., Heyle, A. M., & Ozer, E. J. (1990). Changing and diverse roles of women in American Indian cultures. *Sex Roles, 22*(7–8), 455–476.

Lee, J. A. B. (2001). *The empowerment approach to social work practice: Building the beloved community* (2nd ed.). New York: Columbia University Press.

Livingston, K. (1974). *Contemporary Iroquois women and work: A study of consciousness of equality*. Unpublished doctoral dissertation, Cornell University Ithaca, NY.

Lomawaima, K. T. (1994). *They called it prairie light: The story of Chilocco Indian school.* Lincoln, NE: University of Nebraska Press.

Lowery, C. (1998). American Indian perspective on addiction and recovery. *Health and Social Work, 23*(2), 127–135.

Luna, E. M., Ferguson, D. B., Williams, Jr., R. A., Stafford, R. A., Attakai, A., Carpenter, L. J., Hailer, J. (2002, July). *Impact evaluation of STOP grant programs for reducing violence against women among Indian tribes*: Final Report the National Institute of Justice. Rockville, MD: National Criminal Justice Reference Service (NCJRS). Retrieved February 12, 2010, from http://www.ncjrs.gov/pdffiles1/nij/grants/186235.pdf.

Maguire, P. (1987). *Doing participatory action research: A feminist approach*. Amherst, MA: Center for International Education, School of Education, University of Massachusetts.

Major Crimes Act (1885). 18 U.S.C. § 1153.

Malcoe, L. H., Duran, B. M., & Montgomery, J. M. (2004). Socioeconomic disparities in intimate partner violence against Native American women: A cross-sectional study. *BMC Medicine, 2*, 20.

Mancoske, R. J., Standifer, D., & Cauley, C. (1994). The effectiveness of brief counseling services for battered women. *Research on Social Work Practice, 4*(1), 53–63.

Maracle, L. (1996). *I am woman: A Native perspective on sociology and feminism* (2nd ed.). Vancouver, BC: Press Gang Publishers.

Mello, M. M., & Wolf, L. E. (2010). The Havasupai Indian tribe case—Lessons for research involving stored biologic samples. *New England Journal of Medicine, 363*(3), 204–207.

Meyer-Emerick, N. (2001). *Violence Against Women Act of 1994: An analysis of intent and perception.* Westport, CT: Praeger Publishers.

Mikaere, A. (1999). Colonisation and the imposition of patriarchy: A Ngati Raukawa woman's perspective. *Te Ukaipo, 2,* 34–59.

Moane, G. (1999). *Gender and colonialism: A psychological analysis of oppression and liberation.* London: Macmillan.

Mouradian, V. E. (2004). Women's stay-leave decisions in relationships involving intimate partner violence. *Wellesley Centers for Women Working Papers Series, 415.*

Mullaly, B. (1997). *Structural social work: Ideology, theory, and practice* (2nd ed.). Toronto, ON: Oxford University Press.

Mystique/PlayAround. (1982). *Custer's Revenge* [video game] [promotional material]. Los Angeles, CA: Mahoney/Wasserman & Associates.

Nagel, J. (2003). *Race, ethnicity, and sexuality: Intimate intersections, forbidden frontiers.* New York: Oxford University Press.

Napoleon, H. (1991). *Yuuyaraq: The way of the human being.* Fairbanks, AK: University of Alaska, Fairbanks, College of Rural Alaska, Center for Cross-Cultural Studies.

National Institute for Justice (2000). *Full report on the prevalence, incidence, and consequence of violence against women: Findings from the National Violence Against Women Survey (NCJ 183781).* Washington, D.C.: Office of Justice Programs, National Institute of Justice.

Norton, I. N., & Manson, S. M. (1995). A silent minority: Battered American Indian women. *Journal of Family Violence, 10*(3), 307–318.

Oliphant v. Suquamish Indian Tribe. (1978). 435 U.S. 191.

Parsons, R. (1998). Evaluation of empowerment practice. In L. M. Gutierrez, R. J. Parsons, & E. O. Cox (Eds.), *Empowerment in social work practice: A sourcebook* (pp. 204–218). Pacific Grove, CA: Brooks/Cole Publishing Co.

Peacock, T., George, L., Wilson. A., Bergstrom, A., & Pence, E. (2003, March). *Community-based analysis of the U.S. legal system's intervention in domestic abuse cases involving Indigenous women.* Rockville, MD: National Criminal Justice Reference Service (NCJRS). Retrieved February 12, 2010, http://www.ncjrs.gov/pdffiles1/nij/grants/199358.pdf.

Pelak, C. F., Taylor, V., and Whittier, C. (1999). Gender movements. In J. S. Chafetz (Ed.), *Handbook of the sociology of gender* (pp. 147–175). New York: Kluwer Academic / Plenum Publishers.

Perdue, T. (1980). Cherokee women and Trail of Tears. *Journal of Women's History, 1,* 14–30.

Perdue, T. (1998). *Cherokee women: Gender and culture change, 1700–1835.* Lincoln, NE: University of Nebraska Press.

Rappaport, J. (1997). Terms of empowerment/ exemplars of prevention: Toward a theory for community psychology. *American Journal of Community Psychology, April 15*(2), 121–148.

Robin, R. W., Chester, B., & Rasmussen, J. K. (1998). Intimate violence in a southwestern American Indian tribal community. *Cultural Diversity and Mental Health, 4*(4), 335–344.

Robbins, S. P., Chatterjee, P., & Canda, E. R. (1998). *Contemporary human behavior theory: A critical perspective for social work.* Boston: Allyn and Bacon.

Roche, S. E., & Sadoski, P. J. (1996). Social action for battered women. In A. R. Roberts (Ed.), *Helping battered women: New perspectives and remedies* (pp. 13–30). New York: Oxford University Press.

Rosenberg, M. (1989). *Society and the adolescent self-image* (revised ed). Middletown, CT: Wesleyan University Press.

Rubin (1991). The effectiveness of outreach counseling and support groups for battered women: A preliminary evaluation. *Research on Social Work Practice,* 1(4), 332–357.

Said, E. (1978). *Orientalism.* New York: Pantheon Books.

Said, E. (1993). *Culture and imperialism.* New York: Knopf.

Sale, K. (1990). *Conquest of paradise: Christopher Columbus and the Columbian legacy.* New York: Knopf.

Saleebey, D. (1997). *The strengths perspective in social work practice* (2nd ed). New York: Longman Publishing Group.

Shamai, M. (2000). Rebirth of the self: How battered women experience treatment. *Clinical Social Work Journal, 28*(1), 85–103.

Shepard, M. F. & Campbell, J. A. (1992). The abusive behavior inventory: A measure of psychological and physical abuse. *Journal of Interpersonal Violence, 7,* 291–305.

Shepardson, M. (1995). *The gender status of Navajo women.* In L. F. Klein & L. A. Ackerman (Eds.), *Women and power in Native North America* (pp. 159–176). Norman, OK: University of Oklahoma Press.

Smith, A. (2000). The color of violence. *Colorlines Winter 2000–2001,* 14–15.

Smith, A. (2005). *Conquest: Sexual violence and American Indian genocide.* Cambridge, MA: South End Press.

Smith, L. T. (1999). *Decolonizing methodologies: Research and Indigenous Peoples.* Dunedin, NZ: University of Otago Press / London, UK: Zed Books.

Smith, R., & Loring, M. T. (1994). The trauma of emotionally abused men. *Psychology: A Journal of Human Behavior, 31,* 1–4.

Staats, E. B. (1976, November 23). *Report to Senator James Abourezk: Investigation of allegations concerning Indian Health Service.* Washington, DC: United States General Accounting Office.

State of Arizona (2010). State of Arizona, House of Representatives, Forty-Ninth Legislature, Second Regular Session, 2010-House Bill 2281, Amending Title 15, Chapter 1, Article a, Arizona Revised Statutes, April 2010. Retrieved May 31, 2010, http://www.azleg.gov/.

Tadiar, N. (1993). Sexual economies of the Asia-Pacific. In A. Dirlik (Ed.), *What's a rim? Critical perspectives on the Pacific Region idea* (pp. 219–250). Boulder, CO: Westview Press.

Thornton, R. (1987). American Indian holocaust and survival: A population history since 1492. *Civilization of the American In-*

*dian Series, Vol. 186.* Norman, OK: University of Oklahoma Press.

Thurman, P. J., Bubar, R., Plested, B., Edwards, R., LeMaster, P., Bystron, E., et al. (2003, January). *Violence Against Indian Women, Final Revised Report.* Rockville, MD: National Criminal Justice Reference Service (NCJRS). Retrieved February 12, 2010, from http://www.ncjrs.gov/pdffiles1/nij/grants/198828.pdf.

Tjaden, P., & Thoennes, N. (1998). *Prevalence, incidence and consequences of violence against women: Findings from the National Violence Against Women Survey.* Washington, DC: National Institute of Justice & Centers for Disease Control and Prevention.

Tjaden, P., & Thoennes, N. (1999). Prevalence and incidence of violence against women: Findings from the National Violence Against Women Survey. *Criminologist, 24*(3), 1, 4, 13–14.

Tjaden, P., & Thoennes, N. (2000, February). Prevalence and consequences of male-to-female intimate partner violence as measured by the National Violence Against Women Survey. *Violence Against Women, 6*(2), 142–161.

Tjaden, P., & Thoennes, N. (2000, November). *Full report of the prevalence, incidence, and consequences of violence against women: Findings from the National Violence Against Women Survey* (NCJ 183781). Washington, DC: United States Department of Justice, National Institute of Justice.

Tohe, L. (2000). There is no word for feminism in my language. *Wicazo Sa Review, Fall 2000,* 103–110.

Trennert, R. A., Jr. (1982). Educating young girls at non-reservation boarding schools 1878–1920. *Western Historical Quarterly, 13*(3), 271–290.

Tuskegee University (2003). *Research ethics: The Tuskegee Syphilis Study.* Retrieved March 24, 2010, from http://www.tuskegee.edu/global/story.asp?s=1207598.

Tutty, L. (1993). After the shelter: Critical issues for women who leave assaultive relationships. *Canadian Social Work Review, 10,* 183–201.

Tutty, L. M. (1996). Post-shelter services: The efficacy of follow-up programs for abused women. *Research on Social Work Practice, 6*(4), 425–441.

Tutty, L. M., Bidgood, B. A., & Rothery, M. A. (1993). Support groups for battered women: Research on their efficacy. *Journal of Family Violence, 8*(4), 325–343.

United Nations (UN) (1972). UN Document No. E/CN.4/Sub.2/L566. June 29, 1972. New York, NY: UN.

United States Census Bureau (2000a). *The American Indian and Alaska Native population: 2000 Census brief.* Washington, DC: U.S. Department of Commerce, Economics and Statistics Administration.

United States Census Bureau (2006). *Statistical abstract of the United States: 2004–2005.* Washington, DC: United States Department of Commerce.

United States Census Bureau (2006, February). *Census 2000 Special Reports.* U.S. Department of Commerce, Economics and Statistics Administration.

United States Centers for Disease Control and Prevention (US CDC) (2000). *Building data systems for monitoring and responding to violence against women: Recommendations from a workshop (U.S. Government Printing Office: 2001-633-173/48002).* Atlanta, GA: United States Department of Health and Human Services, Centers for Disease Control and Prevention.

United States Department of Justice (1999). *American Indians and Crime (NCJ 173386).* Washington, DC: Office of Justice Programs, Bureau of Justice Statistics.

United States Department of Justice, Office of Violence Against Women (n.d.). *STOP (Services-Training-Officers-Prosecutors) Violence Against Women Formula Grant Program.* Washington, DC: author. Retrieved June 1, 2010, from http://www.ovw.usdoj.gov/stop_grant_desc.htm.

United States Department of Justice, Office of Violence Against Women (n.d.). *History of the Violence Against Women Act.* Washington, DC: author. Retrieved June 17, 2010, from http://www.ovw.usdoj.gov/stop_grant_desc.htm.

United States Department of Justice, & Perry, S. W. (2004, December). *American Indians and Crime: A BJS Statistical Profile 1992–2002 (NCJ 203097).* Washington, DC: Office of Justice

Programs, Bureau of Justice Statistics. Retrieved May 30, 2010, from http://bjs.ojp.usdoj.gov/content/pub/pdf/aic02.pdf.

Video Game Critic (2008). Atari 2600 Reviews C: *Custer's Revenge*— Grade F. Retrieved March 24, 2010, from http://www.videogame critic.net/2600cc.htm.

*Violence Against Women Act (VAWA) (1994). Title IV sec. 40001-40703 of Violence Crime Control and Law Enforcement Act of 1994. H.R. 3355, P.L. 103-322.*

Violence Against Women Act (VAWA)—Victims of Trafficking and Violence Protection Act (2000) (H.R. 3244). Retrieved June 1, 2010, from http://frwebgate.access.gpo.gov/cgi-bin/getdoc.cgi? dbname=106_cong_bills&docid=f:h3244enr.txt.pdf.

*Violence Against Women and Department of Justice Reauthorization Act (2005). (H.R. 3402). Retrieved June 1, 2010, from* http://frweb gate.access.gpo.gov/cgi-bin/getdoc.cgi?dbname=109_cong_bills& docid=f:h3402enr.txt.pdf.

Wallace, L. J. D., Calhoun, A. D., Powell, K. E., O'Neill, J., & James, S. P. (1996). Homicide and suicide among Native Americans 1979–1992. *Violence Surveillance Summary Series, No. 2.* Atlanta, GA: Centers for Disease Control and Prevention, National Center for Injury Prevention and Control.

Walters, K. L. (1999). *Urban American Indian identity attitudes and acculturation styles. Journal of Human Behavior in the Social Environment, 2*(1–2), 163–178.

Weaver, H. N., & Brave Heart, M. Y. H. (1999). Examining two facets of American Indian identity: Exposure to other cultures and the influence of historical trauma. *Journal of Human Behavior in the Social Environment, 2*(1–2), 19–33.

Weick, A., & Saleebey, D. (1995). Supporting family strengths: Orienting policy and practice toward the 21st century. *Families in Society, 76*(3), 141–149.

West, C. M. (1997). Partner violence in ethnic minority families (No. 95-EXCA-3-0414). *The United States Air Force domestic violence literature review, synthesis and implications for practice.* Washington, DC: United States Department of Agriculture, Cooperative Research Education and Extension Service, University of Missouri, and United States Air Force. Retrieved June

19, 2010, from http://www.agnr.umd.edu/nnfr/research/pv/pv_ch7.html.

Yee, J. (2009). *Reclaiming choice for Native Women.* Retrieved May 30, 2010, from http://www.rhrealitycheck.org/blog/2009/06/11/reclaiming-choice-native-women.

Yellow Bird, M. (2000, February). *Disarming colonialism: A First Nations social worker's manifesto.* Paper presented at the 4th Annual American Indian Social Work Educators' Meeting in conjunction with the Council of Social Work Education Annual Program Meeting, New York, NY.

Yellow Bird, M. & Chenault, V. (1999). The role of social work in advancing the practice of Indigenous education: Obstacles and promises in empowerment-oriented social work practice. In K. C. Swisher & J. Tippeconnic III (Eds.), *Next steps: Research and practice to advance Indian education* (pp. 201–235), Charleston, WV: ERIC.

Yellow Bird, M. & Snipp, C. M. (1994). Native American families. In R. L. Taylor (Ed.). *Minority families in the United States: A multicultural perspective* (pp. 179–201). Englewood Cliffs, NJ: Prentice-Hall.

Young, I. M. (1990). *Justice and the politics of difference.* Princeton, NJ: Princeton University Press.

# Index